# True Story, I Swear It— Maybe

# True Story, I Swear It- Maybe

## True Stories and Tall Tales

### Harvey Cappel

Copyright © 2013 by Harvey Cappel.

| Library of Congress Control Number: | | 2013914901 |
|---|---|---|
| ISBN: | Hardcover | 978-1-4836-8574-8 |
| | Softcover | 978-1-4836-8573-1 |
| | Ebook | 978-1-4836-8575-5 |

All rights reserved. No part of this book may be reproduced or transmitted in any form or by any means, electronic or mechanical, including photocopying, recording, or by any information storage and retrieval system, without permission in writing from the copyright owner.

This book was printed in the United States of America.

Rev. date: 08/19/2013

To order additional copies of this book, contact:
Xlibris LLC
1-888-795-4274
www.Xlibris.com
Orders@Xlibris.com

# Contents

Preface ................................................................. 9
1. A Perfect Car Loan ........................................... 11
2. Bible Donkey .................................................... 14
3. Bum Philips ...................................................... 16
4. Bush Beans Recipe ........................................... 18
5. Chicken and the Egg ........................................ 21
6. Jack Devoti: Fisherman, Inventor, Brewmaster and White Liar ............ 24
7. Dial 1: Standardized Language Selection Menu ........................ 26
8. Electricity for Dummies .................................... 27
9. Fast Pitch .......................................................... 30
10. Feral-Hog Solution ........................................... 34
11. First Day in Heaven .......................................... 37
12. Funeral Home Doors ........................................ 42
13. Ghosts ............................................................... 45
14. Hogs to Slaughter ............................................. 48
15. How to Hypnotize a Chicken ........................... 50
16. Jericho .............................................................. 54
17. Last Deer Hunt ................................................. 58
18. Leroy White ..................................................... 61
19. Love .................................................................. 64
20. Luck Comes From Heaven ............................... 65

21. Man Cookies.................................................................68
22. My Singing Career.......................................................70
23. Odeo's Ark.................................................................74
24. Our Kids' Stories........................................................80
25. Petrochemicals: What, Why and How?......................86
26. Polarization Invisibility...............................................91
27. Rainbow Bridge.........................................................94
28. Report on Hell...........................................................95
29. Sewer Safari..............................................................98
30. Smart First Grader...................................................101
31. Smokey-Water Myth Busted...................................103
32. Snake Stories..........................................................106
33. Steve's Garage........................................................109
34. Toad Suck Fairy Park...............................................113
35. Trillion Dollars.........................................................116
36. Two Funerals...........................................................119
37. Voodoo Woman.......................................................121
38. Weather Scares.......................................................124
39. Work Fun................................................................130
40. X Stuff...................................................................133

## DEDICATION

This book is dedicated to my wife and best friend of fifty-five years, Betty. To date, she is the only one in my life that has had my back 100 percent of the time. Actually there were a few times, when I really messed up, that I'm sure she was looking for a soft spot on my back. Since I'm not normal, having my back during all of my adventures is really something special. Without her, I'm sure that by now I would be dead or in jail. She's been told by her friends, more than once, that there will be a special place in heaven for her because of her life with me. I'd have to agree. But she can't say it wasn't interesting and occasionally fun. And finally—Betty, it aint over yet, hang on.

# Preface

For as far back as I can remember, I have told stories. I can take nearly any situation or event and make a funny story of it. Life is too short to miss out on the fun part. Also for many years I have been writing articles and short stories for various newsletters, newspapers, and even national magazines; some paid but most for free. I enjoy writing to entertain, to inform, and to educate. I have a different view of the world than the average person and not afraid of sharing it. I have, for many years, wanted to write a book but thought that anything I would have to say would be out of date before I finished the book. And then one day, not too long ago, I had an epiphany—life stories, humor, fun philosophy, and basic life lessons don't go out of date. So I wrote this book.

The book is a collection of family stories, tall tales, a few reprints of previously published newspaper articles, a little fun philosophy, and a technical issue or two. Except for a very few of the stories, as noted in the stories, all are original works of mine. The contents are, as you will notice, printed and listed simply, alphabetically. I thought this random arrangement would minimize the potential for one to lose interest and fall asleep reading various versions of the same thing.

My intent in writing this book was not just to make some extra cash, but to put down in writing, in a more permanent form, some of my life's experiences, crazy ideas, and a little technical correctness, for family, friends, and a few others to enjoy.

Please enjoy.

# A Perfect Car Loan

This is about when I was so poor I could have qualified to live under a bridge, except back then we didn't have that many bridges.

My wife was raised by her aunt and uncle, both of whom spoke more Cajun French than English. The aunt spoke only French. My wife had some difficulty with English in the first grade but she has now fully recovered. Her vocabulary at times leaves me speechless; actually not so, but it sounded like something I should include in this story. Truth though is she can hold her own with me or anyone else we know. She's getting better by the day and I'm losing ground.

Her uncle owned a furniture store in town and was known by the family to be rather well off. This proved to be a slight problem when he died broke. Some of the family assumed that my wife inherited all this money. Those that did assume that had to also assume that we didn't spend the money because we were as poor after his death as before. All this background will become relevant as this story progresses.

Just before her uncle's death, he had bought a new 1964 six-cylinder Ford Falcon. He bought it from his nephew, a car salesman. Being a good car salesman, he stuck it to his old uncle, and on top of that he set up the financing to consolidate another bank loan. This made the loan on the car several hundred dollars higher than what the car was worth. This of course was not a problem until his death and the car was no longer needed; the aunt did not drive. So the nephew, who was also the estate assistant executor, decided that the car should be willed to my wife; didn't tell the family about the overpriced car note that was also to be willed to her. I told him we could not accept the car because we were too poor to pay the note. His answer was that the estate would pay the note. Sounds like a pretty good deal then, except that I didn't like six-cylinder anythings, especially Falcons. But we took the assumed-to-be-free car anyway. This sweetened deal was obviously motivated by his need to keep his bum car-selling deal a secret.

Three months later, the car-selling nephew informed me that the estate could not afford to pay the car note any longer. Does that remind you of a car salesman or what? Well, I was at that time working for minimum wage and trying to attend college without any financial help from anyone except my bank that was loaning me money to go to college. It was near the end of the college semester, and that's when I would go to the bank and renegotiate a loan for the next semester; quite often, that included consolidating other loans. So I had a plan to add this car loan to my loan plan and keep the car. However, I still had two or three months before I could do this. Meanwhile I couldn't pay the car note. Lucky for me, I had not had the time or money to change the title of the car to me; it was still in my wife's deceased uncle's name. And by the way, during this time my wife's aunt, suffering from Alzheimer's disease, was unable to communicate even in French. Her mutterings were like a crazy person's and she was in a nursing home.

Now this is where the fun starts. Remember, the car loan is more than the car is worth, and I don't really need or want the car—it's a six-cylinder Falcon. About two months after I had not paid a loan payment on the car, a loan officer of the bank holding the car loan called me. The conversation went like this.

| | |
|---|---|
| Bank guy: | Mr. Cappel, you are way behind on your loan payment and you need to get with the program quickly or else. |
| Me: | Well, if that's the way you feel about it, you need to know that you have the wrong number. I don't own the car you are talking about and if you want it, come get it. It's in my driveway; I don't even want the car. |
| Bank guy: | What do you mean you don't own the car? I was told that your wife was given the car by her uncle. |
| Me: | That's right but as I told you, I don't own the car; the title is still in her uncle's name. |
| Bank guy: | Well, can you tell me how to get in touch with her uncle? |
| Me: | No, he's dead and I can't tell you how to get in touch with the dead. |
| Bank guy: | Oh, I'm very sorry to hear that. Did he have a wife? |
| Me: | Yes. |

## True Story, I Swear It - Maybe

Bank guy: Well, can I talk to her?
Me: I doubt it, she only speaks French.
Bank guy: Well, we can have someone that speaks French talk to her.
Me: I don't think that's going to work.
Bank guy: Why not?
Me: Because she's crazy and wouldn't have a clue as to what you were talking about.
Bank guy: (Without me hearing it) Oh, s—.
Me: Now sir, it's time for you to listen to me and take my offer or else.
Bank guy: Yes, Sir Mr. Cappel, I'm sure we can work something out.
The perfect loan: you have the property but the loan is in the name of a dead person. Try it.

# BIBLE DONKEY

If you have read much of the Bible, you have seen the word *ass* used to describe a donkey. Seems a little odd to see that word in the Bible but there it is, used over and over. People like me, when seeing something like that, wonder why. Is there a story behind this, and if so, what's the story? Now I don't presume to know any more about the Bible than what I read, so this story is just for fun. It does offer an explanation, but I'm sure it really does not truthfully explain the use of ass in the Bible. If you are sensitive about humorous stories about the Bible, then you might want to pass on this one.

One day soon after creation, as the story goes, Eve picked the forbidden fruit from the tree of the knowledge of good and evil and ate it and got Adam to eat it too. Now they were knowledgeable and could see that they were naked. God noticed them hiding amongst the banana leaves and realized that they had eaten the forbidden fruit. God asked Adam about it and Adam said "Eve made me do it" (the beginning of blaming someone else.) When God questioned Eve, she blamed it on the serpent. And when God questioned the serpent the serpent blamed it on the donkey.

Now God was determined to get to the bottom of this, so he went looking for and found the donkey. To God's surprise, the donkey proceeded to tell the truth, the whole truth, and nothing but the truth. The donkey said that the BS stops here; Eve did it and that's my story and I'm sticking to it.

God believed the donkey and went back to Eve for some serious talking. It was a very bad day for Eve and she was, to say the least, seriously mad at the donkey.

Next morning, when Adam and Eve were having breakfast, the donkey wandered by and went into the Garden of Eden. Eve saw this and soon after doing the breakfast dishes went looking for the donkey. Upon finding the donkey, she looked the donkey straight in the eye and said you're an asshole. From that day forward the shortened version *ass* was used to describe a donkey in all the Bible stories.

If this is not true, how do you know?

# Bum Philips

Now I'm sure most of you remember Bum Phillips as the colorful, down-to-earth Houston Oilers football coach. I know Bum but not in a way you would ever guess. I went to high school in Nederland, Texas, when Bum Phillips was there as head football coach. I saw him nearly every day but not at football practice.

I didn't play football in high school because of the following: on my last day in high school as a high school senior, I weighed only 120 pounds; I had to work every day after school; and most importantly, I could not see a future in me practicing every day to get the s____ kicked out of me every Friday night.

My after-school job was at a local drive-in theater where I got an extra seventy-five cents to stay till the last show was over and lock the place up. This got me home on average at about two to three in the morning. Not the best practice for getting up to go to school at about seven. So I rarely got to school on time.

Remember back when, if you got to homeroom late, they sent you to the principal's office; maybe they still do, I don't know. I was always late, so I went to the principal's office two to three days a week for most of my last two years of high school. When I got to the principal's office, they sent me to the head disciplinarian. Remember again, back then, coaches had to work during school hours just like the rest of the teachers, so they handled the discipline and library monitoring; kind of the mean and dumb duties. Bum was the head disciplinarian, so I got to see him nearly as often as his football players.

It would go like this nearly every day: Son, you got to stay in this afternoon to make up for being late. I can't coach; I got to go to work right after school.

Well, if you can't stay in, you got to get some licks. I guess I'll have to get some licks. Okay, go see assistant coach and tell him to give you three licks. So I did and he did and back then a lick was a lick. They used shaved baseball bats and delighted in seeing if a single lick could lift you off the floor. At my 120 pounds, he nearly did. So with a burning butt, I went back to homeroom and started my day with a lesson about being late for school.

Next day, same thing: Bum would say you got to stay in and I would say I can't and the story about licks would get repeated once again. This went on two or three days a week for two years without Bum changing his story or me changing my ways. One might say Bum was severely dense, I was severely stubborn, and I probably hold the world's record for the number of licks received in any two years of school.

One night, during the drinking reception at a banquet, I told this story to a friend and said you would think that Bum would have figured out that busting my butt wasn't working. He replied that Bum could possibly be at a similar party right now telling someone that you would think that Harvey would have figured out that he has got to get to school on time.

A quick note about Bum—in Nederland we had an annual rodeo where Bum rode the pickup horse during the saddle and bare bronc-riding contest. Bum is for real and a real cowboy. But as a disciplinarian, he could have been replaced with a dumb talking parrot.

To this day, and I don't know why, I don't really hold any grudge against Bum. But if I ever meet that assistant coach that gave me those licks, we gonna trade licks and he is going to get his share from me. I weigh 215 pounds now and I ain't afraid of no assistant football coach, especially him.

# Bush Beans Recipe

I know the Bush Beans recipe because that Bush guy stole it from my wife. The original name of the beans is Yam beans. And his dog looks just like one I lost too. Soon as I find out where he lives, I'm going to see him about the beans and check out his or my dog too. This is the true story of the great beans and how they became known as Yam beans before the theft.

I've had a good life and been lucky all of my life. I wasn't born an illegal alien; I was born in Texas with the American dream readily available to me. I, unlike some folks that I know, do not claim to have been smart and hardworking enough to have picked my parents and my place of birth; I just got real lucky. I was also lucky enough to grow up close to the Louisiana border, where the Cajun influence was a dominant factor in the way people enjoyed life and especially good food. Can't understand why all borders can't be that way.

Anyway, food was always a big deal with our families and friends; still is. My wife still cooks as if all our kids are coming to supper starving. Being born and raised Cajun, she can cook and likes to do it; still does. Her grocery shopping for the assumed starving kids—nonshowing, nightly supper guests—basically has made her a professional shopper for the local food bank. She buys way more than we need, so periodically we clean the pantry and freezer and haul it to the local food bank. She doesn't warm up much to the title of professional shopper for the food bank, but I think it's great and I'm glad she does it. She also professionally shops for Goodwill Industries. This is going to get me in trouble even though, to me, it's a compliment.

Weekends meant outdoor cooking and, more often than not, it was barbecue with beans and potato salad. I did the barbecue and my wife did the beans and potato salad. Both the beans and potato salad were special recipes of hers, possibly borrowed from her mother or mine or one of our aunts. Anyway, the beans were really good. I lied a little bit with the title in that I can't tell you the exact recipe of Yam (Bush) beans, but I will tell you enough to get you started on making your own special beans. You see, if I tell all, my wife and that Bush guy will kill me. Not a doubt in my mind as to what will happen to me; good recipes are worth killing for.

So get out your pencil and paper and take notes because I'm only going to say this once. Start with a can or two of cold (room-temperature) pork and beans in a flat casserole dish. Next, add some dark Karo syrup, some white onion rings, and some barbecue sauce (I can't tell exactly how much of each). Cover the whole mess with a single layer of uncooked thin bacon slices. Cook in the oven till the beans are hot and the bacon is well cooked. Try it, and if you don't like it, throw the whole experimental mess away and open a can of Bush Beans. Don't give up though; try again another day. That was the best I could do without getting my wife or that Bush guy involved, and that was just not going to happen; I want to live to eat beans again.

The story on the name, Yam, for the beans goes like this. I, along with a partner, started an engineering business years ago, and we obviously had to hire people to provide the services we sold. One of these new hires was a legal alien civil engineer from Indonesia. He had lived in the USA while going to college, and as most students like him, did not eat well for the four years of going to school. Being of Chinese descent and from Indonesia, however, he did appreciate good food. One day we invited him to our house for supper and an opportunity to eat barbecue, potato salad, and my wife's special beans. That kid thought he had died and went to heaven. We never saw anyone like a food dish like he liked those beans. He begged for the leftover beans every time he heard about us having a barbecue cookout and my wife obliged. True story. This kid's first name was about twenty letters long starting with the letters Yam; so we just called him Yam, pronounced *yahm*, not like the sweet potato. Very soon the special beans became known as Yam beans and still are today.

Now I don't know just how that Bush guy got the recipe, but I do understand why he changed the name; bet he changed my dog's name too. By the way, my dog's name was Trigger. If you ever see that Bush guy with his or my dog, holler *Trigger*. If that dog turns around and responds to that name, please call me. I want my dog back too.

I already got a gang of rednecks and Cajuns working on a plan to get my wife's Yam beans recipe back.

Look out, Bushey, we might be coming to supper one night, real late, with a dog leash and a safe cracker.

# Chicken and the Egg

Here and now, let it be known that the egg came first or they both came at the same time. No way did the chicken come first. I know this by several accounts of facts as will be revealed below.

Having been a little boy and raised on a small farm, I had heard chickens and eggs discuss this very subject. The way this happened was this. One summer when school was out, I was playing in the barn on some hay bales after having just had lunch. The barn was warm, my belly was full, and after some hard playing, I went to sleep in the barn near the wall where the chickens' nests were attached. These were little wood boxes or buckets sized for one chicken each where the hen could set quietly while laying her daily egg. They were up high on the wall, so the chicken snakes couldn't easily get to them but not so high as to keep the hens from getting in. However, just like the rest of life, not everything works out just as you want. So in this case, every once in a while a chicken snake would get in a nest and eat an egg. Now this is important because the chicken snake is part of this story.

As I slept or lay wide awake (whichever is the case, I'm not sure), I overheard a conversation between a chicken and an egg or maybe it was chickens and eggs. Naturally they were debating the age-old question and it went something like this.

Chicken: Well, of course we came first. How you going to get an egg without a chicken?

Egg: Ever hear of evolution and the primordial ooze from the swamp? That's where eggs came from. Surely you wouldn't expect something as complicated as feathers would rise from the ooze?

Chicken: Evolution baloney, we were created just like humans.

Egg: Okay, but from what did you start? Were you created as an egg or as a chicken? Remember, humans have this all confused as well. They keep saying they were created in the image of the creator but they have no idea what the creator's image, at the time, was. The creator could have been blue ooze, and so humans started out as blue ooze and evolved into pink ooze or whatever they call themselves today. So you too, chicken, were more likely created as a simple egg that resembled blue ooze at the time.

Chicken: I never heard of such a bunch of baloney.

Egg: Well, think about it. Would you start with a complicated rooster to make a chicken or with a simple egg?

Chicken: Give me a break, a rooster is complicated? Do you realize that any rooster on the lot could have been a chicken snake meal but for just dumb luck? I mean, he thinks he's hot stuff and self-made when in fact he's no more than the product of luck. I'd like to see any rooster here deal with a chicken snake at the egg level. Seems as how I recall some humans have this same misconception of self-importance.

Egg: Did you forget what we were talking about? Think about this. As an egg, I was created jillions of years ago as part of the swamp ooze possibly in the image of the creator (of unknown image). With jillions of years of evolution, nearly anything is possible. I could have evolved into a chicken and if I did, then the discussion is settled. Creation and evolution are compatible and I (the egg), being the simplest, came first.

Chicken: Good point but can you prove it?

Egg: Well, no and I can tell you why. The problem is, and it is also a human problem, that our brain is still evolving and has not yet reached a level where we can know from where we come. Consider for example the difficulty a cow has understanding algebra. We have the same problem. Actually, there are humans that can't be taught algebra, but that's not my point. You see we, and humans too, still believe that there has to be a beginning and an end when in fact that may not be so. Consider a Hula-Hoop or a simple circle. Neither has a beginning or end and wouldn't even understand our discussion about who came first. They don't have a first and maybe we don't either.

And then I woke up, or at least started to think rationally again. Did the egg win or is it really a Hula-Hoop story (no beginning or end) yet to be understood?

By the way, I ate the chicken and the egg. Neither one has much to say about this human anymore.

# Jack Devoti: Fisherman, Inventor, Brewmaster and White Liar

Jack Devoti was a good friend and all the above, as well as a good family man, father, and retired Grand Prize beer brewmaster. Jack died at ninety-five years young. This story is about Jack and fun folks like Jack. It ends, however, with a surprising story about a very unique invention. Don't stop reading here; the end is worth the effort.

Jack, like most fishermen and many others (golfers for example), was a master white liar. I first met him while living in Bayou Vista, Texas. I was told that Jack could teach me to fish in the marsh adjacent to Blue Heron Street. One day, Jack was fishing in his own front yard in the marsh while I watched and listened to him tell me that the only way to catch fish in the marsh was with a white plastic worm. It wasn't long till he forgot what he had told me and had to reel in his worm to check it. Guess what? It was purple, and the lying continued from there. He thought it was funny; I thought he was full of it. This reminds me of another fish story.

Shortly after I moved to Texas City, Texas, I asked a group of fishermen how to fish in Galveston Bay. They said, first get a large jar of Vaseline, and then put it on your face about a quarter-inch thick. Now I expected I was in for a BS story, but actually they really meant it. They wanted me to wade-fish and use the Vaseline to protect my face from sunburn (long time ago before sunscreen). You just never know when to believe a fisherman. We (storytellers) do, however, have an unwritten rule that covers that. The rule is that if you expect me to believe your story, then you must believe mine; in theory then, no lies.

Now the main reason for this story is to tell you about the origin of the popping cork. For you nonfishermen, the popping cork is the red-and-white cork you see on nearly every fishing line. It makes a popping sound when jerked and that usually attracts fish, hopefully speckled trout. Guess who invented the popping cork? It was Jack Devoti. I have a copy of the USA Patent No. 2741865, dated April 17, 1956. It was called the Jack and Jill float. Jill was Jack's brother. The corks were sold on a handwritten card with rubber bands and toothpicks to hold them on. The center dowel was hand carved. The card reads in part "Attach your favorite plug to the end of the leader, then reel a while, pop a while, and you will be amazed at the results". What's amazing is that jillions of these things have been sold and used. And yes, as with most inventions, the inventor, Jack, did not get rich on it.

So now you know where the popping cork came from and how fishermen lie without lying (probably golfers too). BTW, this rule doesn't apply to politicians—actually, I guess it does.

This story has been reviewed and approved by Jack's wife Pat and daughter Nannette, especially the white liar part.

# Dial 1: Standardized Language Selection Menu

In order to semimediate discrimination, persecution, prejudice, inequity, intolerance, harassment, bullying, potential racial concerns, and to fairly serve everybody we can think of and avoid daily menu change messages et al., the following new and semipermanent standardized selection menu will become effective now and forever more.

Since it is long, all owners of phone products and phone services (except Apple) will be charged only half minutes per minute while making a selection. Apple customers live with it; you bought it. Should you select "repeat menu", you will then be charged at the rate of one minute per minute. We can't, without limit, subsidize and support your ignorance.

Please select one of the following:

1) English or American
2) King's English
3) Redneck
4) Coonass, Cajun for those north of I-10 Louisiana
5) Indian (Native Americans)
6) India Indians (If you have a warrantee or computer question)
7) Spanish (Native Texans)
8) Boston Yankee
9) New York Yankee
10) Japanese (Toyota owners)
11) None of the above (Tea Party Republicans)
12) Repeat menu

# Electricity for Dummies

This is about electricity and a few people that should avoid it if at all possible. The first two are family stories and the last is a work story.

Being a pretty smart guy, my kids and I think I know something about everything. Actually I do but then that's another story. So here was the test of the day. My oldest boy (about eight years old at the time) asked me how to make a magnet. Not taking him very seriously (a big mistake), I simply said you take a lot of wire, wrap it around a piece of metal, and run electricity through it. Next day, that's exactly what he and his brothers did. They took a twenty-five-foot extension cord and stripped all the insulation off it except the plug. Then they got a metal file out of my toolbox and wrapped all the naked wire around it. Oldest boy assigned the middle boy the task of plugging it into 120 volts. Well the sparks flew, set the rug (yes, they did it in their bedroom) on fire, and burned a hole in the wood floor. That was the easy part. When I got home from work, their mother proceeded to do all that same damage to me. Please excuse me for repeating this story later in more detail; it had to go here for the next paragraph.

Now as it turns out, she was to blame. The boy's inheritance of flawed electricity knowledge from her was the reason for the disaster. I know this because of an earlier event that I had nearly forgotten. One day, while at work, my wife called to tell me about the ironing cord that had burned up. This was one of the models that you find today in antique stores where the cloth-covered cord plugs into the back of the iron. Apparently, it had shorted in that plug, burned off, and fell on the floor. I asked her if I needed to call the fire department or come home, but she said no, it wasn't a problem anymore. When I got home, I saw what was left of the cord, about two inches, sticking out of the wall plug about two feet off the floor and still plugged in. I said how did that happen? Did it burn all the way up the wall to the plug? Well, kind of. Every time I hit it with the broom, it sparked and burned a little more. To this day I have not asked her why she didn't just stop hitting it with the broom. If you read this and know her, please don't tell her I wrote it. She still keeps a broom and knows how to use it.

Early on, I worked in an office where one of the employees had the duty of testing materials in a lab behind the building. The lab was a construction shack with two light bulbs in the ceiling on one wall switch. This employee was a real smart aleck. A know-it-all, not well liked by most of us. One day, we decided to mess with him to see if we could prove his true intelligence to be at or below ours. While he was gone one morning, we went into his lab and slightly unscrewed both light bulbs, just enough so they would not come on.

When he returned, we told him about the mysterious electrical problem in his lab and how we had tried everything we could think of the get the lights to come on. We changed the bulbs, we checked the breaker, and nothing worked. After he was done chewing us out for going into his private lab, he went strutting out, mumbling something about how dumb we were about electricity. After an hour or so, he came back in, wouldn't say nothing, just sat at his desk looking at the wall. Time came to go home and we all left for the day. Next morning, we heard him getting some petty cash money to go buy something. He came back with a new switch, put it in, and still no lights. We were loving it. All day he went back and forth doing I don't know what, but still no lights. I know because he would have told us when he fixed it.

We had almost forgotten about the problem till next morning when a big electrical pole truck from our district office, fifteen miles away, showed up in the parking lot. At first, we didn't make the connection and wondered what the truck was doing there with three electricians. As soon as we figured it out, I went outside and told the guys that they sent one too many electricians. It will only take two of you to screw the two light bulbs in all the way. They did and the smart guy stayed mad and quiet for a long time. Be careful with what you think you know because it may not be what you need to know.

I'm sure most of you know about electrons in atoms and some may know about protons as well. Electrons are negative and protons are positive. With equal numbers of each, the atoms are neutral and everything seems to be okay. Now I don't know this to be true, but a friend of mine told me that a small town near where we live doesn't have any protons and another town nearby had some but they were very slow ones. I know the towns well and this just might explain the strangeness of the people living there. If you know anything about this kind of science, I would love to hear from you. I would really like to help these people and will if I can find out what to do about absent and or deficient protons. Maybe reschooling, starting at about second grade, would solve the problem. For them, not me.

# Fast Pitch

Now I assume everyone knows what fast pitch means; but if you don't, it's softball played with the pitcher pitching the ball fast instead of slow, as in slow pitch. This is about my misadventures as a fast-pitch softball pitcher and a fast-pitch softball team manager.

Going into this story, I must confess that I am not a jock. I couldn't even make the Little League team when I was very young. I did go to high school in Nederland, Texas, where the famous Bum Phillips was head coach at the time. Although I had to deal with Bum Philips nearly every day (that's another story), I did not play high school sports of any kind. There are four very good reasons for this: (1) I had to work after school, (2) I only weighed 120 pounds when I went into the Marine Corps, kind of small for sweat sports, (3) I had no jock talent, and (4) I don't chase balls. Speaking of chasing balls, I wonder sometimes if we are looking in the wrong place for the missing link. Considering that dogs and men love to chase balls and apes don't, just maybe we came from a long line of ball-chasing dogs. So how did I become a fast-pitch softball team manager and fast-pitch softball pitcher? The short answer is that we needed both and no one else would do either one.

My day job at one time put me on the supervisor side of smart hardworking folks in a petrochemical plant that had a strong union and strong local company management. That combination was not fun. So while I was there, I tried to make the best of it, and that's where the idea of a softball team (made up of supervisors, company staff, and union employees) came from. I thought, correctly so, that if we could learn to play together, it would be easier and more fun to work together.

## True Story, I Swear It - Maybe

So we put together a team and entered into a local league of fast-pitch softball teams. Unfortunately for us, the league had what's called a ringer pitcher rule. This is a rule that says if your pitcher is famous and well known as being skilled and talented, you couldn't use him as a pitcher. This was unhandy as hell for us because we had two state champion pitchers in our plant. However, we did have a few jocks, so we thought we could compete. No one wanted to manage so I stepped up; heck, what's to do except keep a practice and playing schedule?

Our first game was a disaster. I played right field since I'm the least skilled and that's where the ball rarely goes except for left-handed hitters. I don't remember who was pitching for us but we took the field first. After a couple of rounds of them all batting at least two times, I noticed that the balls kept coming to me in right field. Next thing I noticed was that they were all batting left-handed. What had we got into? We are playing a team of all left-hand hitters. Or was it that we were so bad that they could work us over all batting left-handed. The latter was the truth. Finally after about an hour and a half they called the game on time. We never got to bat. That's a true story and I'll swear on a Bible that it is so.

After that the team unanimously voted to fire our pitcher. That's how I got the pitching job. No one could do worse than what we had, so I would try. I practiced a lot and actually thought I was getting the hang of it. The biggest problem was that it took me thirty to forty minutes to warm up and stop throwing wild pitches. By the time I was warmed up to pitch, I was nearly worn out so that didn't go that well. Still, it was the best we had so we played. Next game we actually got to bat; I think not so much as we earned it, but that the other teams decided to avoid embarrassing us again.

As I said, I practiced pitching every chance I got: with my kids, neighbors, and anyone willing to catch. I started out using my garage house door as a backstop till one of my kids missed the ball and it made a big hole in the door. My wife put an end to that procedure. Back then, it was very common to get together with your neighbors in the backyard to cook and drink on the weekends. This one neighbor, a very little guy with an appropriate nickname that I can't use here, was very talented when it came to drinking beer as I was. I asked him one day, a Sunday afternoon I believe, to catch for me as I practiced. We went out on the street in front of our houses and he squatted down to catch. My very first pitch was a good one, fast and with a rise at the plate. My catcher, being drunker than I realized, did not notice the ball rising and therefore did not move his catcher's glove up. The ball went over the glove and hit him square in the middle of the forehead—knocked him out cold. He finally came too, asked for a beer, and he and his wife explained to me some stuff about my pitching and his catching. Fast-pitch practice is sometimes tougher than the actual game pitching.

There was another problem with fast pitching that I had not anticipated. After my first game of pitching, I came home and found my boxer shorts ripped from one end to the other. How in the heck did that happen? I just blew it off till after the next game when the same thing happened. Being an engineer, this boxer-shorts structural problem seemed solvable, and it was. In case you have ever experienced this and didn't know why here is the answer. After a few minutes into a game, you begin to sweat and after a while you get sweat-wet all over, including your legs inside your shorts. This wet-leg problem causes your boxer shorts to stick to your legs. This is obviously going to be a problem if you try to move your legs very much. So in pitching, immediately after you release the ball during a fast pitch, one leg takes a quick giant step forward—too fast for the shorts to release from your wet leg. The result is a structural failure of the inadequately designed (for fast pitching) boxer shorts; another reason I don't like sweat sports. The failure does, however, make pitching easier the rest of the game and eliminates the requirement of washing the game shorts. I guess I could have switched to jockey shorts, but on decisions about which shorts to wear I'm not that talented. And furthermore, I wouldn't even read this boxer shorts' epitaph if I could write it without reading it.

As the season went on, we settled down to playing with the realization that we were not likely to win a single game this year. I, however, had a secret plan. One of our ringer pitchers, I believed, was unknown to the league. We brought him out one night and won the game against the first-place team. That was dumb, like throwing the frog into the boiling-water pan. The frog will jump and so did they. They protested the win and we lost the protest. It did, however, get their attention.

A final fast-pitch story was the occasion of a fast-pitch tournament we hosted in our town. Being the dumbest manager in our league, I got volunteered to run the tournament. My reputation as a pitcher preceded me, so when our team took the field to play with me pitching, the opposing team had a plan. They knew that sooner or later I would throw a wild pitch and possibly hit the batter. I did, and the batter went down, jerking, convulsing, screaming, and making death sounds to be heard all over that end of town. Their team emptied the bleachers, came running out onto the field, and proceeded to haul him away on a makeshift stretcher of many hands and arms. All the time this is going on, I'm standing on the pitcher's mound posing for the audience as the near killer of one of the other team's players. They thought it was funny; I can't remember what I thought but funny does not come to mind. Unfortunately, this wasn't the end of their fun and games.

One of the teams participating came from a small nearby town known for lacking a few protons. In case you didn't know, we are made up of atoms and each atom contains an equal number of electrons and protons. Now that's the norm, but it ain't always so. When you get an imbalance here, unbalancing things happen. This could account for albinos; who knows? In any case, this town was different. For several years, they killed one of their own about once a month. Many of us would not go there, fearing that we might be mistaken for one of them, or not one of them, and be next on the elimination list. Now that's the origin of this team that's about to take the field for the next game. Now I know all this, so guess what I did when the pitcher laid a .44 Magnum, long-barrel, revolver pistol on the pitcher's mound as he began to pitch? You got it; I did the same as everyone else. I kept quiet and just watched. True story, I swear it.

Well, the plan to enjoy playing together so we could better enjoy working together worked. We, however, did not win a single game the whole season. They fired me as manager and pitcher. Next year, with the jocks in control, believe it or not, they won the city-league championship. This too is true; I swear it.

# Feral-Hog Solution

This story is not really a story. It is more of a public-service information/instruction manual for those that need a feral-hog solution. If, however, you need this solution, it's probably worth the price of this book.

To start with, for those of you that may not know, feral hogs are basically domestic hogs that have gotten out of their pens or cages and learned to live in the wild. They have relearned their wild ways and are somewhat wild and sometimes dangerous. The good news, however, is that they are still about as good to eat as the full domestic hogs. For sure, they can make the pork addition that most hunters use with venison to make deer sausage.

The bad news about the feral hogs is that they are very destructive; they love sex, pregnancy, and large families. Left alone, they are like weeds in a garden, very destructive, very productive, and hard to control. A dozen full-grown feral hogs can destroy a half acre of land in one night. They will root up the grass and leave holes six to ten inches deep, totally destroying the grass or garden vegetables. Although not really nocturnal, they tend to do their damage late in the afternoon and early night when no one is around to disturb or scare them. Since they are wild, they will tend to stay away from people and lights and people noise, but you may not be able to use this alone as a solution. Like any animal that survives, they will evolve to sooner or later learn what is dangerous to them and what is not. So a simple light and noisemaker may not work unless it is a very good recording of barking dogs and gun shots with really bright lights.

Contrary to what you see on TV and read on the Internet, feral hogs are not as smart as most people. Yes, I'm sure you, as do I, know a few people (some are friends) that couldn't pass a hog GED. Assuming, however, that you are reading this, I think it goes without saying that you are not one of them and are smarter than a feral hog; the ones (hogs) I know can't read. Some of the hog hunters on TV, especially those with D-sized bras, I'm not so sure about. They catch one hog per week and? To solve the feral-hog problem, first stop saying the hogs are smart and start some very simple thinking on your own. Feral hogs can be controlled and it's not that big of a deal to do it. Let's first go through all the TV and Internet stuff you see that does not work:

1. By Texas law (and probably most other states), you cannot legally poison, snare, or transport live feral hogs.
2. Shooting hogs at night will get you one hog per night if you're lucky, assuming you can legally shoot where the hogs are. You, however, may have to stay up all night and you won't see the hogs every night. Good luck.
3. Trapping hogs in a small guillotine-gate hog trap will not work. They are in fact smarter than that. They will not go into a small space to eat anything.
4. Dog hunting, although a good sport and probably the reason we have feral hogs in the wrong places (it's believed that some of the hunters transplanted some hogs close to home so they could hunt close to home), will get you maybe one or two hogs per week. Problem with this is that like on TV you will probably have to pay the hunters and force them to kill the hogs.
5. Bright lights and noise. This will work but is limited to very special and small locations. You can't use loud noises in residential areas and you can't practically protect acreage with this system either.

So now that we have exhausted all the wrong solutions, here is the one that will work. I don't claim to have invented this solution (it has been on the Internet for years), but I have tested it and I know it works. It goes like this:

1. Go to your local gun store to get a telephone list of hunters that want hog meat (pork) and are willing to kill (shoot with a deer rifle) a hog before 9:00 AM in the morning. You are going to have hogs to dispose of, and you need to do it early in the morning before the hog lovers find out what you are doing to their lovely hogs.
2. Build a twenty-five-foot-diameter hog fence pen about four feet high with a two-foot-wide swinging and spring-loaded gate. Basically a circle pen with four-foot-high hog wire with a spring-loaded one-way (in but not out) gate. The larger the pen size, the better it will work. Locate the pen as far away from lights, noise, and people as possible.

3. Lock the gate open and feed the hogs hard corn and scrap food (no french fries, they don't like french fries, really) for about two to three weeks.
4. Now set the gate open about halfway and use a small stick to hold it open.
5. Next time they come in to eat, they will knock the stick down when they rub up against the gate, and the gate will close up behind them, usually one or two trapped hogs.
6. The feral hogs are mean and dangerous. They will attack the fence and try to get to you if you walk up on them. That's why you will need a deer rifle to kill at a safe distance.

It's just that simple: feed, catch, kill, and give the pork away till they are all gone. You see, this only requires you to be slightly smarter than a feral hog.

# First Day in Heaven

If you can't take the heat, this might be your fire. You might want to skip this story if you are touchy about your religious beliefs. Remember I warned you.

This is a kind of thought-provoking rambling about heaven. I'm not saying it's so or that it is my belief, only that one might imagine that just maybe.

If you have ever read Mark Twain's *Letters from the Earth*, you will suspect after reading this that I stole some of his ideas. Not so; actually he stole mine. I wrote most of this before reading his book. In any case, if you are seriously religious and haven't read the Mark Twain book, you probably shouldn't. He poses some tough questions about God as I too will do in the following.

Imagine for a short while that you or I just showed up at the entrance to heaven. Obviously, there will be someone there greeting us. I sure hope it's not one of those "self machines" with the first question, "Select a language". Might make me want to turn around and go back to wherever. But, no, this is heaven and there isn't supposed to be anything here we don't like. Yes, there is a very nice person standing at the gate speaking my language. I would like it to be a she so it will be a she.

She greets us with a smile, something to drink (even beer for the rednecks, cowboys, and Cajuns), a place to set, and says I'm sure you have some questions. I raise my hand, put my beer down and say, I certainly do, and I start asking.

Me: Where is God and when will we see him?
Greeter: God is everywhere just the same as it was on Earth. You might say you have already met him or you wouldn't be here. Actually, that's

|  |  |
|---|---|
| | not true as we will see later. But you are seeing all of God that you or anyone else will ever see. It's like seeing the air. He is there but seeing him is not the same as seeing your friend sitting next to you. How could he or she look like you and be everywhere? |
| Me: | Will everything here be fun and okay for me; remember, I don't care much about singing and I do like to drink beer? |
| Greeter: | With a slight exception, yes; whatever you desire will be here for you. You can drink beer all day, fish, hunt, sing in the chore, drive a race car, play with babies, and tell jokes or whatever you want. Your actions will not offend others because others will only see and experience what makes them happy. |
| Me: | You said there was an exception; what's that? |
| Greeter: | Remember that bright light you saw just before entering the gate? That was a sort of screening system that eliminates bad thoughts from everyone. You now are unable to desire or think of anything that would be offensive to God or anyone else here. You just cannot now have a thought or desire that would be unacceptable. So don't worry about that; out of sight, out of mind, or maybe it's the other way around. |
| Me: | Can I ask God a question? |
| Greeter: | Sure can. He does have a pretty big backlog, however, might be several hundred years before he gets to yours. Actually, that's really not necessary. You can't even imagine how many jillion years I've been here answering questions. I don't think you will have a question I can't answer. |
| Me: | How about this. When I was younger, I worked on cars a lot. Every once in a while, no matter what I did, the problem couldn't be fixed. Why did God do that to me? |
| Greeter: | Well to start with, God didn't create cars; man did. So you need to ask someone like Henry Ford that question, not God. God told me one time how disappointed he was in man for creating a car motor with parts that go up and down, spending half its time going the wrong direction rather than one that goes around and around like the wheels it is expected to turn. By the way, Henry is here so you can ask him about your car problem later. Don't expect much of an answer though. |
| Me: | How about the big question, evolution, creation, and the big bang? |
| Greeter: | Well, what about it? |
| Me: | Well, did God create me in his image and if so how do you explain the really old fossils and the big-bang stuff? |

Greeter: Okay, here we go again. Number one, since no one has ever actually seen God, this idea of his image is just a really bad story that keeps getting repeated. God doesn't look like you and never did. So what God actually created, to be a man, was something (we can't even remember what it looked like) that took jillions of years of evolution to finally look like you. Remember time means nothing to God. Number two, as far as the big-bang stuff; it was just a part of evolution. Where you Earth humans get this all wrong is your insistence that there must be a beginning and an end. Ever see the beginning or end of a circle or Hula-Hoop or infinity? Yet all three exist without any problems, don't they? So now you believe you will be here forever and yet you want to know about some beginning and end; get over it, forever is forever, and forever can't have a beginning or end. One more time: consider an ant crawling around a Hula-Hoop looking for the beginning and the end. See?

Me: What about miracles? How did God decide when and to whom miracles would apply?

Greeter: This is another one that you guys got all wrong. When four people die in a car wreck and a baby in the backseat lives, you call that a miracle. Up here, we call that a tragedy. The miracle is the other cars that went by, didn't have a wreck, and all inside were alive at the end of the day. Now there is another way to see the wreck as a miracle (four people got to heaven early), but I doubt anyone on Earth would see it that way. We can talk more about miracles later when we have more time. The subject is pretty complicated and answers are not easy.

Me: What about my wife when she gets here, and my pets that have passed on?
Will they be older than me or younger or what when they show up?

Greeter: Remember what I said earlier. They will be what you want them to be and you will be what they want you to be. You might say we don't have mirrors here large enough to see you and anything else at the same time. For example, you cannot know what your wife sees looking at you and she cannot know what you see looking at her. This is a trick God bestowed on pet dogs. This unique trick makes unconditional love possible. God regrets every day not bestowing this on man. What a missed opportunity for a far better world.

Me: Another big question. What about hell and the devil, and what happed to the criminals and those bring-me-your money preachers?

Greeter: Well, the concept of hell and the devil is again basically a creation of man. The idea of infinite punishment is ridiculous. You would not do this to any of your children and God wouldn't either. We do, however, have to do something about the bad folks before letting them in here. Kind of like the time-out you used on your own kids. It's complicated, but I can give you an example that might help explain it for now. You asked about those money preachers. They're over in another room near here doing pushups. Guess who's counting? You got it; it's those old ladies that lost all their retirement money to those crooks. They are counting and only they know how many pushups are required. The system differs depending on the severity of bad; kind of like the Catholic's idea of purgatory.

Me: I am a little afraid to bring this up, but did you notice that I didn't go to church much?

Greeter: No we didn't notice, so what?

Me: Well, isn't that a problem, I mean like "everyone" says, you got to go or else?

Greeter: I guess you will have to ask "everyone" that question, not God. We do watch what you do when no one is looking, like on Mondays.

Greeter: By the way, speaking of church and Sundays, how many of you got here on the buses we sent? Remember that Sunday when the busses would be at the church at 1:00 PM in the afternoon. There were busses going to casinos, to Disney World, shopping malls, and one going directly to heaven. Remember which one you got on? Remember how many true believers got on the bus to heaven?

Me: I used to tell people that they should be good to old folks because they will get to heaven first and they then can send you some luck, good or bad. Any truth to that story I made up?

Greeter: First time I ever heard of that. Sounds like a neat idea though. I'll bring that up next time I see God. Did you ever see it work? I wonder; is anyone up here really doing that? Come see me when this is over and we'll check out some of the old folks that just got here.

Me: One more question. Is Hitler here?

Greeter: I get that question a lot. Remember one of my earlier answers. You can only see here what makes you feel good and happy. That' really all you need to know on that subject. Whatever makes you happy is the answer for you, but don't assume your desires influence God. He takes care of business, all business. Remember you can't have bad thoughts here and you can't see or know of things you don't like.

Greeter: Let's take a break for now. You will have jillions (I like that word) of years for more questions.

# Funeral Home Doors

I'll tell you right up front here I don't like dead people, funerals, funeral homes, hearses, or graves. I've never touched a dead person and I hope I never do. My oldest son says he's planning to refuse to go to his own funeral; me too. In my story about ghosts, I make a big deal about uncles that scare little kids. I'm speaking from firsthand experience; my uncles made me scared of dead people and funeral homes.

Naturally, I have to pass that on, so one day I did. The occasion was a day when I was babysitting my five-year-old grandson. His parents were at the local funeral home, so my instructions were to drop him off at the funeral home later that day. On the way to the funeral home, I told him some stories about how dead people were dropped off and stored in the various rooms of a funeral home. I went on to say how scared I was to ever go into one of those rooms and how I was very careful not to open a wrong door. Now that I had him scared of opening any wrong door, I proceeded to tell him how to enter the funeral home, which way to turn inside, and how to go down a hall to meet his parents. I went into great detail telling him about which way not to turn on entering the front door, having him repeat the instructions to me more than once. As we got closer to the funeral home, I started having second thoughts about which way was the correct way to turn when going in the front door; again having him repeat the instructions so as to remember and not make a mistake. And then I changed my mind again. By the time we got there, the poor kid was thoroughly confused and did not trust me to know anything about which way to go after entering the funeral home. Even I began to feel sorry for him, but not that much. I had this set up as good as I had ever done. Pulling into the parking lot, we saw his parents outside waiting on him. He was relieved and I was disappointed; all that work for nothing. Bet he won't ever be opening any doors in a funeral home though, just like me. Good practice though for the next victim.

I had this turned around on me one day. A civic club I belonged to borrowed a large tent from the local funeral home for our annual food drive. I was on the committee and assigned the task with another volunteer of going to get the tent. The funeral-home owner was not there, so he left us instructions to get the tent out of a back room from the rear of the funeral home. My helper had been there before, so he knew about the rear door and back room; didn't tell me much though. We opened the door and got the tent box out (there were other similar boxes lying around), and put it into the back of his truck. Now get this. The original tent box had long since been destroyed, so the owner had substituted a temporary transportation coffin box as the new tent box. The box with the tent weighed about as much as an average man (it was a big tent) and we got that box out of the back room, which is also the receiving room for dead bodies, in boxes just like the one we got. I figured all this out just about the time we reached the food drive location. Think I'm going to open that box—not in my lifetime. Somebody else is going to open that box. They did, and it did have a tent in it, thank goodness, or our food drive would have been on the national news. Next year, I was in charge of the food drive; I sent someone else for the tent and again it showed up with a tent inside. I have this to say about this: Don't borrow anything from a funeral home owner if it will fit in a temporary coffin box and don't go the back door for nothing. Also don't go upstairs or get on any elevator. One final note on this: all the funeral home owners I have ever met have a sense of humor and they ain't scared of dead people, so don't trust them.

Belonging to the local chamber of commerce, I was once on a committee that arranged for monthly open-house parties for members. The standard party was usually drinks, snacks, and often free samples of what the business sold. I pushed this free-sample deal because it helped attendance. Then one day, I had an epiphany (sudden realization) that included in our memberships was the local electric power company and a funeral home. Quick committee meeting—these two are exempt from the free-sample deal. Lucky I caught that one just in time. I don't think we were at risk with the electric company, but my experiences with funeral directors told me don't trust them.

I failed to mention this in my ghost story, but funeral homes have got be real important places for ghosts. Remember ghosts come in several kinds, two being of the living and the dead. That being the case, the living ghost must die with the person dying or be transformed into a ghost of a dead person.

In either case, I see this happening in the funeral home probably sometime before the actual funeral; all the more reason to be very careful in a funeral home. Consider the possibility of walking into a room where ghosts were meeting to pay respects to the passing ghost or where that ghost is being transformed from a ghost of the living to a ghost of the dead. Don't take this lightly; a ghost is a ghost with unknown powers and who-knows-what attitude or master plan.

Ever wonder how much it cost for a haircut and shave in a funeral home? Got to be more expensive, wouldn't you think? Scares me just to think about it. I'm going to keep my hair cut, shave every day, and try as hard as I can to stay alive from now on. I'm inclined to say I hope I'm dead the next time I have to go to a funeral home, but then again, being alive and scared might be better than being dead. Not ever having been dead, I can't know for sure. Do you know?

# Ghosts

I know about ghosts. I learned about ghosts in a most unusual way. I ate too many Bush Beans one night for supper, and during the night everything I know about ghosts was revealed to me. I also figured out part of the Bush Beans secret recipe that night. Actually some or none of this is true or untrue. But ghosts are ghosts, and here is all you need to know on that subject.

You may not realize it, but you have probably seen ghosts. They are best seen out of the corner of your eye. Sometime in the past, you probably thought you saw something, a mouse maybe, in your kitchen kind of out of the corner of your eye. That was a ghost, probably a mouse ghost. Ghosts are everywhere. They have to be since there is a ghost for every living human and animal and for humans and animals that have died and are still remembered. Notice I separated animals and humans for those of you that want it that way.

Some scientists discovered the ghost universe of existence recently when they postulated that there are parallel universes. One of our parallel universes is populated with our ghosts. For each of us, there is a parallel existence in the form of a ghost. And for the ghost universe, there is a parallel universe of ghosts of dead humans and animals. You see, ghosts don't die the same time as we do; they go on existing for as long as anyone can remember their parallel human or animal. For example, Abraham Lincoln's ghost still exists but your great-great-grandfather's ghost probably does not, unless he was somebody special and still remembered.

Now that we know the what, what's the why? Why do ghosts exist and what do they do?

Before we get too far into this, notice I have said ghosts exist and have not said they live. For each human and animal, there is only one life but possibly several parallel existences—ghost and who knows what else. Most of us believe ghosts exist mainly for pure pleasure and entertainment. When have you ever heard different? We use ghost stories to entertain pseudo adults by scaring little kids. We use ghost stories to scare stupid adults. I use ghosts to explain some unexplainable happenings.

There, however, must be more to it than that. Since ghosts are as unseen as the wind, could they simply be the wind? Could be; maybe the wind is simply mass movements of ghosts. But if that were so, what would account for the destructive windstorms? Would ghosts do that and if so, why? I don't buy into the wind idea, although some ghost sightings are basically windlike. Ever hit a wind gust while driving on a long stretch of lonely highway; you probable hit a horse ghost or maybe a bear ghost. Actually, I think the wind is its own thing and ghosts just hide in the wind. Makes you wonder though if any are ever hiding in a tornado. Can you tell that I'm struggling with this? I know there are ghosts and there must be a reason, so be patient.

Actually, I know the answer as to why there are ghosts, but I'm going to put off telling you till the end of this story so that you can guess yourself. The answer, to me, is obvious so let's see if you get it like I did.

Before we postulate as to why ghosts exist, let's explore their existence. Let's look at our manifestation of imagination to see some of the many forms of ghost. What did you think of my "manifestation of imagination" phrase? Let's look at that for a moment. Did you know that radio is more perfect than TV? Radio provides a perfect image of whatever we hear about. TV provides a real image. Consider this: the radio announcer tells a story about a woman with the dimensions of 36-28-36. You see this as a very attractive sexy lady, when in fact, as seen on TV, this could be a ninety-year-old grandmother with serious uplift-and-restraint undies. You see now how manifestation of imagination works? We can imagine anything we want and in special ways, actually experience it and enjoy it or hate it and fear it. That's how ghosts exist. They are what we imagine. So now back to the many forms of ghosts.

The most common form is the scary ghosts. These live in haunted houses; typically, houses where someone met an untimely and cruel death. Or maybe more than one person died. The ghost(s) may be the killer or the killed or both. The thoughts of what happened there stimulate the imagination to the point of creating the scary ghosts. These ghosts usually go away when the house is destroyed. Where else could they go?

Another popular ghost is the one the deranged (like me) adults use to scare little kids. These can take on any form but usually are not killers or gruesome types. They are just old and ugly with mean-looking faces. They threaten bad but never really do anything bad. They are easily destroyed by the child's mother as soon as she becomes aware of the stupid uncle who created them in the first place. But soon we create new ones, don't we? Children, beware—uncles are ghost creators.

The good ghosts are the after-death reappearances of loved ones. Usually older women see these. They see their mothers or grandmothers or lost dear friends and even pets. Remember there are ghosts of pets as well as humans. These ghosts exist as long as the one that sees them lives.

And finally there are the friendly ghosts like Casper McFadden. You didn't know Casper had a last name? Good thing you bought this book. Now, the truth be known, *the* Casper isn't really a ghost. Casper was invented in 1930 by Seymour Reit and Joe Oriole. He was a friendly ghost but could find no friends because the uncles had scared all the kids about ghosts. In case you didn't know, this bothered Casper so much that he tried to commit suicide by lying on a train track. That worked about the same as cutting air in half. Good thing though because he finally became known as a friendly ghost. Certainly there are other friendly ghosts. I hope so.

So now back to the question of why are there ghosts. The answer is easy and obvious. It's entertainment. It's perfect images and predictable stories and it's all free. Ball games, picture shows, car races, and plays all cost money, and we have no control of the outcome. Ghosts are free and ghost stories are exactly what we want them to be, and every part of the manifestation of our imagination is perfect. Life needs more ghosts and ghost stories.

Oops, I nearly forgot about the Bush Beans recipe. About midnight, after eating the Bush Beans, I woke up with a loud burp. It's dark Karo syrup; that's one of the ingredients. I can't tell you how much Karo syrup it takes per can, but I did figure out how many beans it takes to make a can of beans. It takes one can. Well? What?

# Hogs to Slaughter

We were on our way to an old-engine-and-tractor show in Indiana when this happened. Our friends were in a motor home like ours following behind us. He was always behind because in those days, diesel engines smoked and puked out a fine mist of unburned oil. In any case, I always like to lead. Neither one of us however knew exactly where we were going, so when I passed up the place we were going to, he saw it in time to turn.

Now, in case you didn't know, turning around a thirty-eight-foot motor home with a car being flat towed behind is not fun. It is actually harder than turning around an eighteen-wheeler because with the car behind, you can't back up. So you have to think like you are in an airplane with no reverse. So down the road we went looking for a real wide spot to turn this monster around. My wife was getting nervous, and I was trying to talk to our friends on the CB radio when I saw opportunity. Up ahead, I saw a building on the left with a large empty parking area in front. As I approached it, an 18-wheeler in front of me obviously had the same idea; he wanted to turn around also. No problem, I just followed him into the parking lot close behind as he headed out to the road again.

Now this was where the problem started and the stuff hit the fan. He didn't exit the parking lot but instead started to back up. He saw me close behind and started signaling for me to back up. I couldn't back up. After he gave up on hand signals, he got out and tried to explain to me in very plain English that I needed to back up. I too explained to him in very plain English that I couldn't back up without disconnecting the car, which I didn't want to do.

He got back in his cab and proceeded to back up anyway, only centimeters from the front of our motor home.

That's when we found out that he had a load of hogs, and he needed to back up to the building to unload them. Now the hogs either knew what awaited them or they, like my wife, were getting real nervous about his backing that big hog trailer so close to our motor home. He backed a few feet and the hogs squealed, then he pulled up and stopped and the hogs squealed, and he kept doing this, getting closer to the building door while just missing our motor home and with the hogs squealing. My friends kept calling on the CB and my wife had long ago left the front seat so she would not have to witness the crash and hogs everywhere. Needless to say, the truck driver was not happy and getting more so as he tried to get the truck parked at the unloading door.

Finally he did it and, lo and behold I was clear and could pull out to finish my turnaround. Not wanting to deal with him, I hurriedly started to drive off. Just as I was about to pull out onto the highway, I saw him in my rearview mirror trying frantically to stop me. I was thinking, he wants to settle this problem physically. I'm not much of a fighter, but I have had some Marine Corps training, so I'm no runner either. If I had to get my butt whipped, I guess I just had to because I'm not running; I stop.

Just as I was trying to get out the door, my wife was trying to get in. Somewhere in this ruckus, she had left the motor home and I didn't know it. I was about to leave her at the hog slaughterhouse with a mad truck driver. As it turned out, he didn't want to whoop up on me as much as he didn't want to deal with my mad wife. Hard to say which was worse, without the actual experience of the whooping. I can tell you this: I will never follow a hog truck that closely again, and I sure as heck won't leave my wife at any hog slaughterhouse again. I now count heads, people, dogs, mice, everything in the motor home before driving away.

All things considered though, I'm sure I came out of the ordeal much better than them poor hogs. I wonder—did I later in life eat one of those hog's ribs? Hope not.

# How to Hypnotize a Chicken

Really, I'm not kidding. I can do this and I'm going to teach you how as well. I've known this unique skill nearly all my life and kept it a near secret all this time. With this story, however, I am going to tell all. Unlike the Bush Beans secret recipe, this will no longer be a secret. You too will now be able to hypnotize chickens even if you still can't cook Bush Beans.

Before I reveal this well-kept secret, let's reminisce a bit about life on a small farm. I grew up on a small farm with three cows (two for milking and one bull being raised for meat), one hog, fifteen chickens, 148 rabbits, two geese, one dog, two cats, and me. At eleven years old, I pestered my daddy till he taught me how to milk the cows. At twelve years old, I pestered my mother to tell my daddy that I was too young to be milking cows. Well, as you know, when the cat's out of the bag there's no putting it back, so I milked cows till I left home the day I turned eighteen. Went to Marine Corps boot camp and after about two days, I wished I could go back home and milk cows. Again, I let the cat out of the bag and couldn't get it back in.

In case you don't know, cow milking is a twice-a-day job every day including Saturdays, Sundays, holidays, and vacation. You can't leave home without them cows. My daddy worked shift work (seven-to-three, three-to-eleven, and the hated eleven-to-seven shift—graveyard shift as they called it), so we traded milking times morning or afternoon depending on his shift. After milking the cows, there were other farm chores to do like filling the cow's water trough. This took several minutes that gave me time to get distracted and forget to turn the water off. I can't remember how many times I was awakened at midnight, jerked out of bed by a furiously mad daddy having just come home from work to find most of our property underwater. Back then, it wasn't against the law to abuse children, so I got abused.

I got even with him one night though. I had a little brother who had one of those spring-suspended hobby horses. This was a little plastic horse held by four springs, one on each corner of a steel frame about three feet high. Now I didn't do what I'm about to tell next. If I did and admitted it here, my daddy would come back from the dead and abuse me again, or at least meet me at heaven's door. Daddy, I didn't do it. Here's what happened. We had a back porch with a screen door and steps going to the backyard and barn. One day, for some reason, I couldn't milk the cows in the afternoon, so my daddy had to do it at midnight when he got off work. He did not like that and neither did the cows. The night was cold and there may have been ice on the back porch; don't know for sure about that. In case you don't know, hand-milking two cows means you carry two large milk buckets full of hot water to the barn. The hot water, of course, is to wash the cow's teats before milking.

So here goes my daddy, late to milking, probably mad and running out the back door in the cold with no lights to see, carrying two near-full milk buckets of hot water. After the bottom step, he steps into and on top of the spring-sprung hobby horse my brother had left at the bottom of the steps. Now he went up and down and the buckets of hot water went with him, hot water everywhere, and I can't even finish this sentence with the laughing tears in my eyes. Years later, I could still hear my daddy tell how many times that horse bucked him off and stomped him before he could get loose. With no light to see what was trying to kill him, he had the experience of his life on that hobby horse. I didn't get to see it or I would not be alive today; I know he would have killed me before I had any chance to blame it on my brother. I can tell you this though: if you or I could have seen that show, it would have been classic. It almost is just thinking about it.

Long after this near-death episode was over, when I was in the eighth grade, me and my daddy had another one of our one-sided discussions about milking cows. I had learned enough mathematics to do an economic analysis of cow milking versus buying milk. I had, I thought, figured out a way to end my hated cow-milking chores. It was costing us more to get milk and meat from our cows than what we could buy both from the grocery store. My daddy was smart and after seeing this, I was sure he would sell the cows and stop all this foolishness. Remember sometime ago when they introduced the new math in schools. We didn't understand it, but it was the new way even if we didn't like it. Well, guess what? There was another math that I had never heard of; it was my daddy's math. Needless to say, the next morning and for a jillion more, I milked cows.

Now why did we have 148 rabbits and how did we get them? The answer to the second part of that question is easy: I started with two rabbits and nature set in. I was actually trying to raise them to sell as Easter bunnies and for meat. They are really good to eat, like fried chicken. My selling skills, however, could not match Mother Nature, and pretty soon all of my eight dollars a week I made cleaning a local cafeteria went to feeding the rabbits. I did try to sell them, and here's how and why they didn't sell.

You have to understand some more about small farming before I can tell the details about selling rabbits for meat. Cows make manure and it has to be dealt with. Our neighbors would pick it up and make large piles to later be used as fertilizer. My daddy had a different idea about that. Since we did not need all the milk two cows could produce (we sold some), he saw no reason to pay extra for milk-producing cow feed. He instead bought what was called horse and mule feed; it was cheaper. Now, this feed had a lot of whole grains in it that did not get digested; it came out nearly the same as it went in. So the cow patties had lots of wheat and corn mixed in, perfect food for chickens. The chickens would spread the cow patties and eat the grain, so we did not have to pick up the manure and we did not have to buy chicken feed. Three cows could support fifteen chickens and fifteen chickens could clean up after three cows. You might say my daddy was way ahead of his time. I sure liked and supported his system.

So what has this to do with selling rabbit meat? Remember, the neighbors had piles of manure, more than they could use, so some was for sale. My friend (the neighbor's kid) and I would then go together around town knocking on doors selling cow manure and rabbit meat. Now think about it; would you want to buy your meat from the same guys who were shoveling cow manure? We sold a lot of cow manure buy not many rabbits. I have tried to use that lesson in my life: for me, it's easier to sell bull s\_\_\_ than it is to sell meat. You bought this book, didn't you?

One more farm thought and then I'll tell you how to hypnotize a chicken. Growing up on a farm, you get to see the real world of food. It isn't always so clean and neat as you see now in the supermarket. Take, for example, milk: the first thing you do with it after bringing it into the house is strain it through cheesecloth. Yes, in a barn with flies and a cow's tail full of cockleburs slapping flies while you milk stuff happens. Think that's bad? Not really.

You see, drinking this impure milk allowed us to make our own antibodies. If allowed, your body will make antibodies and guess what, they know you, and they know exactly what your needs are. Your homemade antibodies are not a compromise that kind of works for everyone but doesn't exactly match anyone. Your homemade antibodies don't have side effects and will always get the exact dosage just right. Except for a hernia operation, I don't remember going to a doctor till I was about forty years old. I think we were designed to get a little germs with our food to keep the body tuned up for a big germ attack; maybe so, maybe not? By the way, they pasteurize (heat it to kill germs and bacteria) milk now. This obviously assumes the milk still isn't super clean when it gets to the milk tank. Too bad. We may be missing the opportunity to make our own antibodies. I thinking about now that if a doctor reads this, he will think I'm full of it and he will probably be right. But it might be so.

Now the part you paid for. This secret alone is probably worth the price you paid for the book. Actually, I've changed my mind and I just can't be telling everyone how to hypnotize a chicken. Just kidding, but you have to promise this; do not tell anyone how to do this. Make them buy the book.

Get a chicken. Bet you already knew that part. Get someone to protect you from the roosters; they will attack to protect the hens. With both hands hold the chicken on the ground on its back looking up. As soon as the chicken settles down, hold the chicken's head in your left hand with it looking up into the sky. With your right hand and index finger, point your finger at the chicken's eyes, about three inches away. Once the chicken gets focused on your finger, remove your left hand. The chicken will now be lying on its back looking up at your finger. Slowly pull your finger away from the chicken. That sucker is hypnotized and will lie like that for about four or five minutes. Now, if you really want to make a scene, do this to all the chickens in the chicken yard. Get a picture and send it to me—I've' done it before but never thought of getting a picture. Be prepared also for the chicken owner to blame fewer eggs on you for what you did. Been there, done that.

A final note: don't try this on your kids or wife. It won't work.

# Jericho

If you are not having fun at work, quit. Life is too short to suffer eight hours a day just for money. Work can be fun especially if you have somebody like me on the job. Even as a company owner, I did my share of fun stuff nearly every day.

Now if you are one of those folks who think you have to look and act professional all day every day, then this is not for you. You most likely will not find it to be humorous. In fact, you might wonder about my sanity and think bad thoughts about me. That would bother me about the same as a high-velocity right cross from a piss-ant ghost. Hope you didn't read this before you bought the book. Don't take it serious; remember I'm trying, even now, to have fun and mess with your mind so that your troubles will have to take a ticket and wait.

I once owned half of a company that employed about a hundred people, of which about forty were in our home office where I worked. Even though I owned half the company, I work alongside our employees, doing the same work as they did. We worked together on various projects as necessary to get the jobs done that we were getting paid to do. As you might guess by now, some of these employees were really unique and fun-loving folks.

One guy in particular—I'll call him Jericho to protect him from my following abuse—was more than average fun. Jericho was an alcoholic who could really enjoy drinking. I have had my days as well. Get over it, it's the real world, people have problems, and some of us understand and try to help. Jericho finally solved the drinking problem and I am proud to say our understanding and patience with him paid off. Jericho is okay today.

Now for some Jericho stories; this first one is a little off-color, so if you are a little queasy about eating, you might want to skip this one. I expect many of you, like me, have had at least one hemorrhoid operation. Anyway, I did and everyone at work knew about it and why I was off work. On the first day I could go back to work, I was in the kitchen getting ready to leave to go to work. My wife was cooking bacon and I happened to notice a small piece that looked like a small donut or guess what—it looked like what I would imagine the cut-off of a hemorrhoid operation would look like. I couldn't resist it. I made me a string necklace and put the piece of bacon on it. Now this thing looked like the real thing. So off to work, I went planning a first-order-of-business visit with Jericho. I walked up to his desk and we exchanged the usual words about my operation and my return to work. Jericho did not notice the necklace, so I asked him if he had ever seen what they cut off in a hemorrhoid operation. He said no, then I showed him the bacon ring on my necklace; he nearly fell out of his chair getting away from me and it. I assured him it was simply a piece of meat and extremely sterile, having been butchered in a hospital operating room. To prove that it was safe, I ate it. I can assure you that this story pales in comparison to the joy of witnessing Jericho's reaction in person. Now you probably think there is something wrong with me using such a gross project just for a laugh. So be it. It was one of the funniest things I've witnessed in my life. Unfortunately, it probably contributed to Jericho's drinking problem at the time.

Now you have to understand a little about Jericho to appreciate some of this humor. Jericho did his share of stuff, so he wasn't the innocent employee that we took advantage of. An example of his nature was his call-in one morning being late for work—as is the normal case for most alcoholics—to say he was late because of the severe snowstorm in his town. This was July in south Texas; his town hadn't seen snow, even on its coldest day, in more than ten years. What could I do? I couldn't fire him: he was too much fun.

When our kids were young, we camped out a lot. On one of these trips, as we were breaking camp and getting ready to go home, one of the kids found a tarantula spider. This dude was about five inches in diameter with its legs out and real aggressive; it would stand on its rear legs and look at you as if ready to fight. Needless to say, we caught it, put it in a box, and brought it home. When we got home we started thinking about a small cage to keep it in and something to feed it. Being midsummer, we had lots of what we call June bugs (small beetles) so the feeding was no problem. The dude ate several of the June bugs and finally quit and settled down in its new home. Next morning, we went to check on the dude and it was dead. We were shocked at what had happened and had no idea what killed it. But it was still dead.

Now is where my "not-normal" mind takes over my body and made me think of Jericho. It might be dead, but to me it was not as yet used up. I picked the dude up and brought it to work. As usual, Jericho was late so his desk was just sitting there waiting on me. I put the dead tarantula in one of the drawers of his desk. He came in later and I waited all day for him to discover the spider. By the way, tarantulas are not poisonous and have a very difficult time biting large objects like humans. I would never do anything to kill one of my employees especially a valuable one like Jericho. Nothing happened all day, so I basically forgot about the spider and went home after work. Next day, I decided to force the issue a little. I had in the back of my mind the thought that Jericho had found the spider and was not reacting to it so as to throw me off guard for something he had planned for me. So anyway, I went to his desk and started asking him questions to try to get to bottom of this event. Finally, I accused him of having seen the dead spider and trying to mess with me. He insisted not so and pulled out the drawer to prove it. At first, all we saw was his junk which I started moving around to find the dead tarantula. To my great surprise as well as Jericho's, the spider was in the drawer and alive and mad as hell. We both jumped back as if we had seen a giant spider, because we did. That sucker was not dead. After some effort, we got the spider out of his desk and to this day I don't remember what we did with it. But this prank was on me as well as Jericho. Later, I learned that tarantulas' gorge themselves when eating and go into a one—or two-day coma while digesting the food. That dude was not dead; it was in a natural coma. The lesson here is if you feed a tarantula, be prepared for a death and resurrection.

This last Jericho story occurred long after Jericho left our company and went out of my life for several years. I actually thought he had died from his drinking problem. Anyway, one day my wife asked me to get tickets to a play called *Beauty Shop*. She had seen a TV advertisement about the play and wanted to go see it. I'm not much on plays but I am a lot about doing what my wife says, so I got the tickets for us and another couple. The play was in a nearby big city, so when the time came to go we went early to make sure we could find the theatre.

Now to understand the rest of this story, I must tell you that Jericho is black. He has no problem with that and neither do I. However, you must understand that anything from the most common, milk-toast normal is fodder for fun. So get over it if Jericho being black means anything wrong to you. We are good friends and color means nothing to either of us unless we can use it to have fun.

So as we were walking to the theatre, we began to notice a very unusual number of black folks heading the same way we were. As we got to the theatre, it became obvious that the play *Beauty Shop* was intended for a black audience. Okay, so what? We had tickets (we were white) and it wasn't against the law for us to go to a black play. We went in and found our seats; sure enough, we were the only white folks in the theatre. I'm not going anywhere. In my opinion, I belong here with good folks like me, so we settled down to get ready for the play to start. To my left there were several seats vacant but not for long. I was sitting next to the vacant seats so when the people began to work their way to them, I watched. Before I knew it, the fellow working his way to the seat next to me was Jericho. I couldn't believe it. Not only was he alive, but here in a theater with several hundred people, Jericho gets a seat next to me. The first thing I said to him was, Just in case there is a problem, you will speak up favorable of me, won't you? Jericho was remarried and had been without an alcoholic drink for several years, had a good job, and was happy. Hadn't planned on that good happening, but I was glad to see Jericho and glad he was alive and well. I know that wherever he is today, he is enjoying life to its fullest just like me.

# Last Deer Hunt

On my last deer hunt, I didn't go hunting but did bring home two deer and only fired one shot. Without a doubt, this was the best success I'd ever had at bringing home the meat. Most of my life, I hunted deer the old-fashioned way, on free paper-and-sawmill-company properties. We didn't have deer feeders then, and because we had not taken care of the deer as we do today, there were not many deer to be seen. In fact, it was not uncommon then to go a whole year without even seeing a deer. My last encounter with killing deer however was between these times of nearly no deer and the pick-the-one-you-want we enjoy today.

Now as I said, I didn't go deer hunting that weekend. What I did was take my three boys and a friend of mine with his two boys to spend a weekend in deer country near a friend's deer lease. We did not have permission to hunt the lease, but I brought a deer rifle anyway. My friend and his kids had never seen a deer in the wild, so I thought just having the kids see some deer would be a fun weekend.

A little side story here; on the way to the lease, we stopped to eat lunch, and I believe everybody ordered fried shrimp. My middle son is like me—he can eat more than most humans and will eat nearly anything. Keeping in mind also that during these times we did not go to restaurants to eat (no money), so my son had never seen a fried shrimp with part of the tail shell still attached. You've got to be guessing what's coming next. When we were all finished and getting ready to leave, I looked at my son's empty plate and asked, Where's your tails? You know it; he said, What tails?

Getting back to the nonhunt trip; after getting to the little town and checking into a motel, we took a late evening drive out to the lease. As expected, we saw several deer. While still on a back road on the way back to town, we found a small buck deer in the middle of the road. We had just passed this place a few minutes earlier going to the lease, so the deer had obviously just died there. Actually, it had committed suicide or something like that, having fallen from a cliff just above the road. It was below freezing, so we just field dressed the deer, tagged it, and put it in the trunk of the car. One deer, on a nonhunting trip, and no bullets fired—first time for me.

Next morning, we went back to the lease, but didn't see anything till we were well on our way out on an old dirt road, when one of the kids hollered there's a deer. I couldn't see it but stopped the car anyway to see if he really saw something. And yes, several kids saw it but I still couldn't. My rifle had a scope on it, so I used it to see the deer, and sure enough about a mile away in another county there stood an eight-point buck. With the rifle propped on the car, I could see it clearly now. To this day, I don't know why I did what I did, but I aimed about twenty inches above the deer's shoulder and pulled the trigger. Before this, I had never shot anything I didn't expect to kill and eat. There's no way I could have expected to hit that deer but I shot anyway. The kids all hollered, You got it. I said no way, but I couldn't see the deer anymore, so I naturally assumed that the deer just ran off after hearing my shot. I said, Let's get back in the car and go home. They said no way. I was outvoted by all the kids and my friend. I said, Look, guys, if you want to go down through that valley and up that hill to waste your time looking for that deer, go ahead on, but I'm not going. My friend and several of the boys took off. After some time, maybe thirty minutes or so, I could see them signaling and hollering that they found the deer. Now you have to understand, at this point, this so called friend of mine. He worked for me and delighted in tormenting me with practical jokes, and he was a master at it. This fool was simply trying to get me to make that useless trip through the valley and up the hill like they did. I threatened to fire him and beat him up in front of his kids if I claimed that hill and there was no deer. They insisted, so the rest of the kids and I went down the valley and up the hill. Sure enough, there was the shoulder-shot dead deer. After about two hours of hauling that deer down the hill, through the valley, and back up the hill to the car, we put it in the trunk and went home.

To this day I can't figure out how I killed that deer at that distance. I did win a second place trophy in a three-hundred-man rifle-shooting contest in the Marine Corps, but still. I do have one theory though that is probably right. Someone else that was much closer to that deer and essentially hunting on private land without permission, like us, shot at the same exact time I did and he killed the deer and I simply put a round in the ground. Problem for him, however, was that he didn't know about us till he saw my friend and the kids coming after him or the deer. Wisely, he left the deer and me with a tall-tail deer story.

# Leroy White

Now Leroy White is not this fellow's real name, but anyone knowing him except himself will know who this is about. Now he would never guess that this is about him, and that's why he is fodder for my fun.

Seriously, Leroy is a good friend and has been for a long time. Leroy is a man's man. He is always outside or in his garage doing man stuff. He can fix anything without a clue as to how it works or should work—kind of a magic touch. I have that magic touch from time to time but I usually do know a little about what I am doing. Magic and luck are hard to beat though; rather have them than skill or smarts any day. Well, maybe.

I first met Leroy on a car-club outing. We all had old cars and would caravan to some small town to spend the weekend just eating, shopping (ladies only), kicking tires, drinking a beer or two, and just trying to stay away from the TV. Now Leroy was on this trip prematurely, to say the least. He did have an old car, but he had not yet bothered to assure it would run after leaving his driveway. Wasn't very long on our trip till Leroy had a car problem and then another and then another. Seems the trip was about working on Leroy's old car. He put a confirmation on the FORD that said "Found on Road Dead", if you know what I mean; it was a *Ford* product. The next-to-last failure did begin to show Leroy's real genius at fixing stuff. The fuel pump failed. This being an old car, the local parts store in the very small town did not have a replacement pump. No problem; Leroy just bought an electric pump and some tubing to convert the old car to electric pump operation, without the standard electric pump safety features, I might add. However, it did work. This by the way was a fix on the way home while we all waited in our cars on the side of the road.

Finally, we were all running again but just for a few miles when I saw Leroy's car stopped again—the last failure of the trip, or at least the last one I saw. I told my wife that this guy must be one of those people that like to meet strangers on the road. They watched TV and played on the weekends (instead of doing normal maintenance on their car) so that during the week, they could experience the adventure of meeting strangers on the road as needed to help maintain and or fix their car. I said, he wants to do this, so why should we interfere? Let's go home and leave him to his social adventure. And we did. A few days later, I found out that his last stop was a flat tire and naturally he did not have a spare. What really took the cake was that the flat tire had his very own pocketknife stuck in it. He had left his pocketknife on the fender of his car when he was cutting tubing for the electric fuel pump. After driving a few miles, the pocketknife fell off and he ran over it. At least he didn't lose his pocketknife.

At that time, I was the editor of our car-club newsletter, so I wrote a story about this idea of meeting strangers on the road and how some folks preferred this to the normal reliable transportation the rest of us preferred. I didn't use Leroy's name, but it was obvious I was writing about him. I didn't know Leroy very well at that time and assumed I didn't want to know him, so I didn't care if the news article peed him off. It didn't, and in fact, I learned later, after we became good friends, that you could not make Leroy mad no matter how hard I tried.

By the way, for you car-club guys: want to know how to successfully caravan? Caravanning without a police escort is always a problem, with other cars cutting in and passing. The way to control this is to put all the black cars up front and have everyone turn on their headlights. Now everybody thinks it's a funeral and will stay back and out of the way. It works; we did it a lot.

As I stated earlier, Leroy could fix anything, and part of the reason for that was that he had a different definition of fix than most of us. I used to say that if Leroy heard a corpse pass gas, he would declare it alive and well. He once had a two-cylinder outboard motor that to my knowledge never ran on but one cylinder. I never was able to get him to accept the fact that the motor was not running right. He was easy to please and hard to make mad. In a real (complimentary) sense, Leroy is like a puppy dog. He rarely found fault with anyone no matter how stupid or mean they were.

After we both completed our old car-club adventures, we started flying radio-control model airplanes. Actually, he started crashing model airplanes;

was what we did. I had a full-scale pilot's license but only limited knowledge of radio-control models. Leroy started this first and I told him to join a local club and pay his experience dues—you know, messing up in front of everybody, picking up the pieces, and trying again. He didn't want to do that; he wanted me to teach him to fly and he was going to learn without any model-airplane pilot expert's help. So we did. He built a small inexpensive trainer-type airplane, which we took to a local public park to test on the ground. Now all I could do was talk to him because he had the controls. Finally, the day came when we decided to let it get airborne. It flew, went straight up, and then straight down. Either he didn't listen to anything I said, or what I said was all wrong. The airplane was trash. Later, we both joined a club and finally got to flying, but Leroy never bought another new airplane after that. Everything he owned from that crash day was just slightly better than junk, which he couldn't fly nor could anyone else. Actually, it wasn't quite that bad but close to it.

One day he brought a new (very well-used) airplane to the flying field and asked me to fly it first, as it was bigger than anything he had flown. I had by that time actually learned to fly, at least, better than him. So after inspecting it, I told Leroy I didn't think it was in good enough shape to fly. But remember what I said about Leroy: if it could pass gas, it was in good shape, according to him. So we got it in the air and all was well for a short while till I rounded one corner, and from very up high, the airplane started straight down. The controls I needed to stop this descent didn't work, so I could see the inevitable—a serious crash. I had time to ask Leroy if he wanted to hold the controller while it crashed, but he said no. Remember, I said I could fly better than Leroy; however, I wasn't skilled enough to know to shut off the engine power before the crash. The airplane managed a negative three-feet altitude, requiring a shovel to dig it out of the ground. Not all bad though because something like that is fun to watch, especially if it's someone else's airplane.

Leroy and I had many good days learning to build and fly radio-control airplanes. Actually, we played with old cars and fished a lot too. He moved away, and because of some health problems, we don't do much together anymore. I still fly the models and he still talks about it, but it's not the same. Too bad; maybe again someday if the preachers are right and we don't mess up.

# LOVE

Author unknown, but I suspect a very young person.

1. When someone loves you, the way they say your name is different. You just know your name is safe in their mouth.

2. Love is when you go out to eat and give somebody most of your french fries without making them give you any of theirs.

3. Love is when my mommy makes coffee for my daddy and she takes a sip before giving it to him to make sure it tastes okay.

4. Love is what's in the room with you at Christmas if you stop opening presents and listen.

5. Love is when you tell a guy you like his shirt, and then he wears it every day.

6. Love is when Mommy gives Daddy the best piece of chicken.

7. Love is what makes you smile when you're tired.

8. Love is like a little old woman and a little old man who are still friends after they know each other so well.

9. Love is when your puppy licks your face even after you left it alone all day.

10. When you love somebody, your eyelashes go up and down and little stars come out of you.

11. You really shouldn't say "I love you" unless you mean it. But if you mean it, you should say it a lot. People forget.

# Luck Comes From Heaven

If you never thought about being good to old folks, this might make you reconsider. You see, on average, old folks will get to heaven before you do, unless of course you are older than them. Even in this case, who knows for sure? Better be safe than sorry.

Seriously, have you ever thought about luck and why some folks have good luck and some folks have bad luck and how luck is a part of life? Except for a few games like chess and checkers, nearly everything in life and every competition involves some luck. One might consider forgetting education, homework, practice, and experience and just depending on luck. Probably not a good idea, since in most cases luck plays only a small part on the outcome. An unlucky but skillful player will still always beat a dumb butt. But luck does count and one would be unwise to discount it completely.

So then, how can I plan for and use luck to help me through life? I believe there are at least two ways. The first being as I mentioned at the beginning of this story: depend on luck from heaven. Work on it by being good to everyone you think will get to heaven before you. Don't forget about bad luck; that too may come from heaven. There is another way, however. You can buy good luck. Really you can. Consider someone like me that figured out this heaven connection many years ago and spent most of my life being good to old folks, many of which are now in heaven. I have, you might say, a very large company of luck-senders up there just waiting on my needs. I have so much luck now that I can actually give some away or even sell it. I'm not kidding. I have already done this.

Years ago, when I legally drag-raced every weekend, I used to sell luck to other racers. You see, at a drag race in a given class, there may be, say, 128 competitors. On the first round of racing, pairs of drivers race each other with one winning and one losing. At the end of that round, there would be sixty-four winners left. Doing the math, you can see that the ultimate winner must win seven rounds of paired racing. So racers talk about the number of rounds won and I sold luck on a racing-round basis. You could buy one round of luck or two or seven, whatever you wanted. The price was whatever you wanted to pay, and it was a money-back deal. For example, if you wanted really good luck, you might buy seven rounds of luck at ten dollars per round, keeping in mind that winning the race could bring you up to one thousand dollars. So for seven rounds, you pay a total of seventy dollars to win one thousand dollars; and if you lost you get that losing round's and the remaining round's money back. How can you lose? It worked, and I did sell it to at least to a few fools. I was often asked about the price and what would be a fair price. My answer was you get what you pay for. If you want to buy one-dollar luck, don't expect much.

One year, during my racing career (really just amateur sport racing), a new national racing organization came to our track and asked me to help them get started. I knew a lot of folks and car-club people, so I could help them get the word out and I did. On the third year (they came to our track once per year), they got rained out three times. Knowing the owner, I made him an offer. If you let me in free every year and pay my racing entry fee, I will use my luck to keep the rain away. It was a hard sell, but being, again, a money-back deal, he went for it and I raced the next ten years free and he had no more rainouts. True story.

After years of this success, I offered this deal to another national racing organization. The deal with them was to pay me one thousand dollars for the weekend race, which was about a million dollar-deal if everything went well with no rain problem. This was in the form of a letter to the president and board of directors (owners of the racetrack). The letter, which made the offer, also had a paragraph explaining that one might consider that a person that could prevent the rain could also make it rain; no threat, but just a thought. I found out later from one who attended the meeting that it was actually discussed at the meeting a week before the event and rejected as a foolish prank or worse. The weekend of the race it rained, and the million-dollar deal went away and about a hundred-thousand-dollar loss took its place—a total rain-out disaster. Again, later I found out from one who attended the weekend meeting during the rain that my name was mentioned with some idea of blaming me for the rain. Now think about that. They did not believe that I could prevent rain, but some did believe I could make it rain. Dumb butts should have paid me the one thousand dollars. If it didn't rain, they would net $999,000 out of the million. And if it did rain, I would have given them the one thousand dollars back, and the outcome would have been the same as if they never saw me. True story. One might want to think about a deal like that if one comes your way.

So be good to old and sick folks and let me know if you want to buy some luck.

# Man Cookies

When I was a little boy, I remembered eating cookies that my mother cooked. I remembered that I liked them and that they were different than store-bought cookies. These cookies were very hard, tough, and didn't have any foo-foo stuff on them. You could put a few in your blue-jeans pocket carry them around all day and they would not break, crumble, melt, or get foo-foo stuff on your jeans. Unfortunately, my mother died before I had the good sense to get the recipe, and my two sisters and brother failed as well.

My wife and I, being pretty good cooks, thought we could figure out the recipe, so we tried for years without success. Finally, one day I had an epiphany (I like that word). I suddenly realized what it was that made those cookies different. Our family was kind of poor when I was a little boy, so when I asked my mother to make cookies, she did it the cheapest way she could; after all, I was just a kid and anything sweet would probably do. To make cheap cookies you just need flour, sugar, butter, vanilla flavoring, and milk. You don't really need the expensive eggs and baking power. Guess what? When you leave out eggs and baking powder, the cookies do not have air bubbles and do not rise. They are flat, hard, and durable, but they still taste good. They are hard as rocks, so you need good teeth to eat them. They are not for wimps or little girls, that's why they are called man cookies.

Now I was going to give the recipe here but decided that just in case this book didn't work out, I might need the cookies to work on my being the next Bush Beans guy or the next Famous Amos with my great cookies. I will, however, give out enough information so that if you are a good cook, you might be able to come close to duplicating my great cookie recipe.

Here's the secret.

1. Start with a sugar cookie recipe.
2. Leave out all ingredients that might make the cookies rise; eggs, baking powder, baking soda, etc.
3. Roll the dough out to one-eighth-inch thick.
4. Use a cookie cutter to cut in two-inch circles; no animal shapes for men.
5. Cook at 350°F for about twenty-five to thirty minutes till slightly brown.
6. Don't put foo-foo stuff in the cookies.
7. Don't put any sugar or foo-foo stuff on top of the cookies.
8. Consult your doctor before giving cookies to kids under five years old.

If you are old enough, enjoy the memory; if you are young, make a new memory.

Do not tell anyone this secret. Make them buy the book like you did.

# My Singing Career

For those of you who know me, this is going to be the most unbelievable story in this book. I've kept it a near secret till now. It is, as all of my stories, true. This one is really true.

When I grew up—correction, when I was younger, my heroes were the tough guys in the movies played by John Wayne and later by Clint Eastwood—remember, according to my wife, I'm still growing up. And later, I also wanted to be Dale Earnhardt, race-car driver and intimidator. As a young boy, very young, I thought all dogs were males and all cats were females. I also thought that only girls were supposed to sing songs. Unfortunately for my wife and kids, I didn't get over all of that. I'm pretty sure I was wrong about the dogs and cats, but the rest is still stuck in my mind somewhat.

This singing thing kept me from singing all my life. Before the events of this story, I had never even sung happy birthday or the national anthem out loud; can you see John Wayne or Dale Earnhardt singing? So why and how would I ever have a singing career? You will soon see, although it was a very short career.

One day while riding in my car, I heard a song being sung by Ray Price that really got my attention. At that time, I was reading a charm book at the request of my wife and in the mood to be good for a while. The occasion was just before our forty-fifth wedding anniversary and the name of the song was "You're the Best Thing that Ever Happened to Me". To me, that kind of said it all about my wife. I had been, for years, having trouble buying anything for my wife's birthday and anniversary; I mean, we have a little money and she has credit cards. What can she want that she doesn't already have? So I got this great idea for a forty-fifth wedding anniversary gift.

## True Story, I Swear It - Maybe

A little background first. Nearly every Friday night, we go to the Alvin Opry in Alvin Texas. This is a Branson, Missouri-type show where they have a house band and local performers—some amateur and some professional—show up and do their thing. The audience sits in theater seats and there is no dancing or alcohol served. The music is vintage Gene Watson country from about the '60s through today, actually; Gene Watson still has a band and performs. The owners of the Opry are Gene and Sue Hofford. Gene Hofford and most of the house band members have had some past serious, full-time careers in country music before giving up the traveling to settle down to a local weekly show. The weekly show is not unlike a family jam session where everyone knows nearly everyone. The band members are very family friendly and the audience is family folks and about 70 percent repeat. Many of us have standing reservations where we only call if we aren't coming, and we always get the same seats. Family stuff like before TV. After several years of regular attendance, my wife and I have become very good friends of the owners Gene and Sue Hofford.

Given that, I decided that I would, on the occasion of our forty-fifth anniversary, get on stage and at least fake sing that Ray Price love song to my wife. Gene and Sue were accommodating, so the plan started developing. At first, it was going to be me lip-syncing with Gene offstage singing. Now, you have to understand that Gene is a musician and that makes him different than most folks. Knowing Gene, I did not believe I could count on him to remember what he was supposed to do on the special night, so that offstage lip-syncing idea was dropped by me. All the time we are trying to figure out how to do this, I was practicing singing while riding in my car with a cassette of the song and a tape recorder. I would sing, record, listen, and then try again to correct my mistakes. It was tough, much harder than I had imagined. Next idea was to get a karaoke tape or CD and have it played while I sang. This didn't work because I couldn't find a karaoke tape or CD of the song. So one night there at rehearsal, I tried singing with the Ray Price tape playing at very low volume. They said it sounded like I was singing off key, whatever that means. At this time, I had been practicing in my car for about six weeks and getting better every day. So the next plan was to rehearse with the band. Two problems ruined this. First of all, they said they didn't have twenty years to work with me, and second, some of the important band members were not going to be in attendance on my special night.

The date was coming soon, and I didn't have a workable plan except for me to sing without the aid of the band, a cappella. I was, however, still practicing and getting better each day, so it seemed possible. Now, another important fact that made this possible is that at my stage in life, I am no longer intimidated by anyone or anything. The thought of getting on a stage in front of a live audience to sing for the first time in their lives, for normal folks, would have been devastating. Not for me; that part of my brain apparently died sometime back.

Gene said okay, let's do it, him assuming I could at least sing. Remember now that this was a complete surprise to my wife and the friends that came with us that night. And it really was. Then finally, onstage, I talked to the audience and went through a few thoughts about what I was about to do and how impossible it would be for anyone to expect me to do it. I expected my wife wanted to leave or at least hide under her seat. Later, I learned from one of the regular singers that my comedy routine was superb but my singing was severely lacking in current or even future value. Most of the band had no idea what I was about to do, had not rehearsed, and didn't know the song. I asked them to play what they could but, if so, do it at a very low level since it would surely distract me. Near the end of the a cappella song, the very talented fiddle player started playing, and I think it might have helped a little. In any case, I did it and got a stand ovation. Notice I said stand (singular); one guy stood up as he applauded. Thinking back now, he was probably getting ready to go to the restroom.

My singing was about what you would have expected from John Wayne or Clint Eastwood, but it was sincere and went over well; a no brainer since most of the audience was good friends. I couldn't do wrong and didn't.

It was a night I will never forget, and I think that will be the case for a few other folks as well. The song title "You're the Best Thing that Ever Happened to Me" said it all that night.

If you have never heard the song by Ray Price, check it out; the song's words are as good as the title.

I have been asked many times to do it again, or something like it. My answer is that it was a once-in-a-lifetime event. If I do it again, the singing occasion of my forty-fifth wedding anniversary would no longer be a once in a lifetime event. So that night was the beginning and end of my singing career. And the world is a better place because of my singing retirement decision.

As of this writing, my wife and I recently enjoyed our fifty-fifth wedding anniversary, and on the Friday closest to that date we went to the Alvin Opry.

My wife was nervous as a cat in room full of working rocking chairs. She did not trust me when I told her I had no plans for any surprises that night. I kept my word and did nothing exciting that night; wish I hadn't said that. Remember I was protecting the once-in-a-lifetime treasure.

Now, I'm working on a writing career, which will probably start and end with this book—maybe another once in a lifetime treasure. Have you ever had a once-in-a-lifetime fun experience? If not, well, it's time you did. We're all waiting.

# Odeo's Ark

My God has a sense of humor. I see proof of that every morning when I shave. From what I see in the mirror he/she must have had a fun day making me, probably still laughing today when thinking about it. And by the way, my God doesn't kill either. If your God is not like mine, you may not want to read this. It's up to you.

This is a story about a modern-day Noah's Ark. Don't know if this actually happened, but if it did it might have went down something like this.

The lower portion of the state of Louisiana is almost like another country. Folks living south of Highway I-10 and even more south of Highway 90 are called Cajuns, or as I know them, Coonasses. It's okay; that's not a bad word. My wife is one and proud of it. The working-class Cajun considers the term *Coonass* as a badge of honor, a certain ethnic pride, and not insulting, so long as it comes from another Coonass or, as in my case, one that's friendly with or related to a Coonass. But just so I don't upset you Northerners and otherwise uninformed, I will refrain from using the term *Coonass* for the rest of this tale.

Somewhere in this Cajun region of South Louisiana, it matters not exactly where, lived a couple by the names of Odeo and Francine Babineaux. My spell-check is having big problems with these non-American words and names—I told you it was like another country. Anyway, Odeo, like many other Cajuns, was a shrimper (he catches shrimp for a living) and a boat builder (he builds shrimp boats). He speaks Cajun French better than English but gets along pretty good with both languages. Odeo is a good Catholic and goes to church every Sunday, or Saturday if he wants to sleep in on Sunday. Francine is in the choir and usually goes on both Saturday and Sunday. Odeo is as like the Bible's Noah as anyone could be. So it's no surprise that one day God called on Odeo for a special project.

The initial conversation went like this:

God: Odeo?
Odeo: Who said that?
God: It's me, Odeo. God.
Odeo: Is that you, Maurice? You know better than to play games with God's name.
God: It's really me, Odeo. I need you to build an ark.
Odeo: Now I know it's you, Maurice. If Francine hears your BS-ing me with this God and ark thing, you're not going to like what she does. Remember she prays every day and talks to God.
God (with a loud clap of thunder out of a blue sky): Odeo, do you want a little touch of lightning next to get your attention?
Odeo: No, sir, I believe it's you and you want me to build a what?
God: An ark. Remember the Noah thing? I want to do it again.
Odeo: You can't be serious; you want to kill everybody again?
God: I'm not going to kill anyone; I never have killed anyone. That Bible story is all wrong about that point. Think about it, anyone can walk faster than any rising water from rain. I couldn't kill anyone with rain if I wanted to. I just wanted to get their attention and I want to do it again.
Odeo: Okay, then what's this ark all about if not to save people?
God: It's for the animals, Odeo. Not all animals can survive forty days of high water. Think about a frog or crawfish trying to swim for forty days above a bunch of hungry fish or elephants, not knowing which way to go and having to tread water for forty days. The ark is for the animals, Odeo.
Odeo: Okay, I'm in, but I don't have a cubit tape measure. You're going to have to give me better instructions than what's in the Bible.
God: Odeo, just measure the animals; I never told you how big to build a shrimp boat, did I?
Odeo: Okay, and I guess like the Bible I need to plan on two of each right?
God: Odeo, I hate to use the word *dumb* but you are making me wonder about you. Give me a break, Odeo. Really, do you think two ants will do, or two bacteria, or two fleas. By the way, do you know how to tell a male bacteria from a female bacteria and more importantly, how could you possible expect the two you choose to like each other enough to reproduce?
Odeo: This ark is really going to be big, isn't it?

God:    Remember the loaves and fishes story? You make the ark and I will make sure it's big enough.
Odeo:   Yes, sir, I'll start first thing in the morning.

Now Odeo is thinking harder than he ever did before, and all of a sudden he realizes he has another big problem. He is going to have to build the ark in his front yard, and that means he will have to explain it to Francine.

This is how that went:

Odeo (from out in the yard, he hollers): Francine, I am going to build an ark.
Francine: Odeo, you didn't shrimp again today, did you? You and Maurice been drinking all day, right?

Odeo:   No, I mostly have been talking to God.
Francine: Now, I know you have been drinking and you been drinking that cheap wine that Maurice buys, I bet.
Odeo:   All I can say now is just watch tomorrow morning, and next time you talk to God ask him if it aint so.

So Odeo begins to build the ark and during construction has a few conversations with God.

One was like this:

God:    Odeo, I can't tell the front from the back of that ark. Do you know what you are doing?
Odeo:   Am I right, God, the ark isn't going anywhere?
God:    Well, yes, I suppose that's right.
Odeo:   Then why does it need a front or back?
God:    Good point, Odeo.
Odeo:   By the way, just how big is this flood going to be? As I understand it, the first one just flooded the land that was known, and that obviously did not include Louisiana, but now practically all the earth land is known. Going to flood the whole earth?
God:    No, Odeo, I never made that much water, and if I did, where do you think it would be now? It's just going to be Louisiana and Missouri, just two examples. I wasn't even going to do Missouri, but you know them, they have to be shown, so I'm going to show them.
Odeo:   How you going to keep it from spilling over into Texas?

God: Remember who I am? And besides, some of East Texas is just like South Louisiana, so what's the problem?

Odeo: No problem, heck, I'll help with that plan. The more of Texas we can wet on, the better I will like it.

God: Odeo, that kind of thinking is why I'm doing this. Do you want to tread water for forty days or ride in the ark?

Odeo: Oh, you misunderstood me. I only meant that to water their gardens.

God: Odeo, do you realize who you are lying to? Get back to work.

As time went on and the ark began to appear as a very large boat in Odeo's front yard, it began to attract attention. Odeo lied and tried as best he could to keep the real project a secret, but one day while he and Maurice were celebrating with a jug of cheap wine, the cat got out of the bag. At first he tried to get Maurice to keep it a secret also, but that didn't work; Maurice told his wife. Pretty soon, everyone in South Louisiana found out about it. At first they thought it was just a bunch of bull. However, as time went on, they began to really believe. More importantly, they began to plan. Being experienced in planning for hurricanes, they kind of looked forward to the day; maybe we can have a Noah's Ark flood party. This planning got so serious that Odeo began to think the flood was not going to work; these Cajuns were too tough and smart to let a simple flood ruin their day. Even the insurance adjusters from other states were calling and asking Odeo about when this was going to happen. Florida remodelers and roofers were calling too.

This needed to be reported to God, so the next time Odeo talked to God, it went like this:

God: I see you are getting close to done, Odeo, looking good.

Odeo: God, I think we got a problem, or more to the point, I think you have a problem.

God: What's that, Odeo?

Odeo: I must confess. I let the cat out of the bag and all of South Louisiana knows about your plan to flood the state.

God: Well, that's unfortunate, but since we are nearly ready to do it, I don't see a problem. I mean, like in a few days they were going to find out anyway.

Odeo: God, do you realize that every Cajun has at least one boat?

God: So?

Odeo: I mean, we could have just had them collect a few animals and not even had to build this giant ark. Also, they love being in their boats.

| | |
|---|---|
| | With this flood, they won't even have to get their wife's approval to go boat riding and fishing. I don't think they are going to have a problem with this flood. |
| God: | But it's going to be deep and for forty days. |
| Odeo: | They are already planning to use their shrimp boats and shrimp nets to catch crawfish. They are planning parties. They are planning to get new houses out of this deal with their insurance. |
| God: | Now you have me concerned. Do you think the whole deal will be a failure? |
| Odeo: | Well, I think your plan to get their attention is not going to work. As far as a failure, I'm beginning to think that if you call it off, they will consider that a failure. |
| God: | What about the North Louisiana folks and those in Missouri? |
| Odeo: | Can't say. What they hear from us, they never believe anyway, so I think they will be greatly surprised. How about this; go ahead and do it, then we will have a lot of good times, get some new houses (*lay-zay lay bon ton rule-ay*—let the good times roll), and you can at least get those Yankees' attention. |
| God: | I'm not thinking that will be a good idea. |
| Odeo: | You do realize that if you call this off, I will be in big trouble. I mean no one will ever believe me again. |
| God: | I never knew that to be a problem for you in the past, but if you say so. |
| Odeo: | I don't presume to know your business, but rather than calling it off completely, how about, say, a ten-day rain, just enough for the flood parties and a few insurance claims? Heck, go ahead and do forty days on Missouri if you want to. |
| God: | Odeo, do you remember anything about hell? You are really getting into sinful thoughts. |
| Odeo: | Oh no, sir, I was just supposing. You do what you think is best. |
| God: | I think I'll just call this one off and start again with some fellow in New York. |
| Odeo: | Sounds good to me, but good luck on finding anyone in New York who can build an ark. How about asking him to buy one and I'll put mine on eBay? |

And that's the way it went. Odeo did suffer some embarrassment about the whole deal. He did, however, finally sell the ark. Some rich Texan bought it; said he wanted to use it to take his cows out in the ocean to make them seasick for purging like the cleaning (purging) of crawfish before you boil them. Said it would make a super-clean prime beef that he could sell at a really high price. If you happen to see it (the ark) in the Gulf, you might want to stay upwind of it.

As of this writing, I haven't heard anything about any New York fellow building an ark or super-clean prime Texas beef either for that matter, have you?

# Our Kids' Stories

If you have read very much of my writing, you probably by now have an opinion of me that includes the words crazy, dumb, heretic, atheist (not true), funny (hopefully), an intellectual bully (bragging now), and a few other words that don't now come to my mind. My point in the previous sentence is to have you suppose that our kids just might be a little different and difficult to raise. You would very definitely be correct.

Following are a few stories that made life fun and interesting for me and the fun-loving crazy kids my wife and I survived with or hope to. The firstborn, being the oldest, was often the leader and the expert at blaming one of the younger ones, two other boys and a girl.

My wife and I were married about a year before any signs of babies started coming. However, when the door opened, out came a litter in a hurry. The firstborn, after nine months and a few days, took all day being born. Second one came pretty darn quick about twelve months later and the third came about fifteen minutes after that; then the last one, almost born in our car, came about eleven months later. In just about two years, we went from no kids to four kids all still in diapers, real diapers by the way.

Getting back to the twins, which happened in a time when a pregnancy of twins could not easily be detected. We didn't have the sonograms and oftentimes the heartbeats could not be confirmed as being two instead of one. That was our case. Also, that was a time when a man was a man—can you see John Wayne in a delivery room (oh, I'm going to get in trouble for this)? Back then, the men stayed in the waiting rooms while the wife and doctor did the baby delivery thing. After the boy (second son) was born, the nurse came out and informed me of the blessed event. I called our parents and friends and told them we had another boy. The normal procedure then was to wait another half hour or so till your wife was brought out and transferred to a room. I had done this before, so I knew the procedure and timing. I patiently waited while studying for an upcoming college exam. After about an hour, I began to be a little concerned. Finally, after a too-long wait, a nurse came out asking for me. This really concerned me until she informed me that my wife just had a little girl and both wife and baby were okay. Of course, I was really lost now, so I asked her if she had the right me. She said yes. I told her that my wife had had a boy about an hour ago, to which she informed me that she knew a boy from a girl and just saw my wife deliver a girl. Finally, she said, I'll go see about the mix-up. When she came back, she said, We had one of each and the mix-up was because the first delivery team thought they were finished with the birth of the boy and had gone on to other duties. A little later, a second team found out my wife wasn't done and they didn't even know about the first birth, or that's what it seemed like to me. Poor as we were, I was delighted with the twins, thinking we would be kind of famous and be getting some free stuff like milk and diapers—didn't happen. What did happen was that I had to make all those telephone calls again (nickels in a coin telephone that I couldn't afford) and not only convince them that we had had twins but also that I was not drinking.

Being poor with four kids and me trying to work and go to college, we didn't get to go anywhere for entertainment. That's what messed up me and our kids. We learned to have fun messing with each other's minds. For example:

One day, when all the babies were on the floor after finishing eating, I asked them if they knew how they could hear. The oldest pointed to his ears and the others followed suit and pointed to their ears as well. I said no, that's not so. I then asked them to point their index fingers at me to see if they could hear what I was saying. They did and said they could hear very well. I then asked them to hide the ends of their index fingers in the holes on the sides of their heads, their ears, and see if they could still hear me. Said no, so there's the proof; you hear with the ends of your index fingers. Sometime later, maybe while in high school, they finally figured out I was wrong. By then they had figured out a lot of other stuff about me as well.

I know this is stupid, but I have to tell it anyway. If you have twins, you will appreciate what I'm about to tell. Our twins were boy and girl. I don't know how many times my wife and I have had to tell people that they were not identical twins. True story, I swear it.

The boys grew up very slowly, like me (my wife says I aint there yet) and not normal. One day, I bought them a brand-new swing and slide set and spent most of a Sunday putting it together. I came home from work the following Monday and soon noticed it was not in the backyard where I had built it. I asked my wife what happen to the swing set, to which she answered, I haven't a clue. When I went to the backyard to look around, I found it in all its original individual pieces on the ground in the grass. I wanted to kill a few boys, but instead I worked into the night and built it again. Next day Tuesday, I came home and the damn thing is missing again. Same story, they took it apart again. Believe it or not, this happened a third time, after which I took advantage of the then lack of laws protecting children from child abuse. I seriously abused them.

Later on, that same summer we were in the backyard when I notice the smell of gas. I checked out the gas meter to see if it was leaking. Remember, gas meters have a large plate on the front and another on top. Very soon, I noticed that neither plate had any screws holding them on. I looked down on the ground to find all the screws neatly stacked in a pile. Lucky for me and the boys, they did not know the plates were removable, and now the plates were being held on only by sticky gaskets. I carefully put it back together and abused them again. After that, I checked that meter ever day till they left home to live in another place.

Another dangerous adventure involved the making of a magnet. I know I told part of this story before, but the additional details here make it worth telling again. One night, while I was watching TV and enjoying a beer or two, one of the boys interrupted my pleasured moment by asking me how to make a magnet. Not wanting to stop drinking or watching TV and really not knowing exactly how to make a magnet, I told them that you just get a piece of metal, wrap some wire around it, and run some electricity through the wire. They then left me alone and I forgot about the whole deal. Not smart on my part. My kids do nothing without a reason. They don't ask questions without something on their mind. They were going to make a magnet next day after school and do it the way Daddy said. They got a large file and a twenty-five-foot extension cord out of my toolbox. They stripped all the insulation off all but about ten inches of the twenty-five-foot extension cord. They wrapped all this loose copper wire around the file and took into their bedroom where they had a 120-volt wall outlet. I really need my wife to describe what happened next, but to this day I can't talk about this to her without getting into trouble all over again. Actually, there was a worse day when the kids dropped about a dozen nonincubated but badly rotten eggs on the bedroom carpet—another science project failure. In any case, the oldest got one of the younger brothers to plug the experiment into the wall socket. How they survived, I don't know, but a file-sized section of the carpet didn't. From then on, when they asked me a question, I threatened them with child abuse if they did anything with the answer without consulting me.

My daughter was not without fault. She was just like the sister I grew up with. She delighted in finding ways to get her brothers in trouble—didn't take much talent to do that. I do remember one thing about her that entertained all of us. She was very small, a little over five pounds at birth, so she was really cute to watch when she first started walking. What was really fun was to watch her walk when she was mad. She would close her eyes and walk toward her bedroom, miss the hall doorway, and walk straight into the wall. She did it more than once, and just maybe, that could be the cause of her abnormal ways today. She teaches kindergarten and first grade now—those poor kids. Some nights when we couldn't find anything else to do, the boys and I would make her mad so we could watch the funny show. True story, I swear it. Please don't tell my daughter or my wife about what I just said about me and her brothers making her mad.

Speaking of her, one day when she was older, we had a pool party at our house for her and her friends. One of the friends was a well-built jock that was throwing everyone in the pool. He bragged about how no one could throw him in, and for a while he did manage to avoid getting chunked in the pool. He bragged a little too much in front of me and that was not a good idea. I went into the house and came out with a bull whip and proceeded to show everyone how I could pop it. If you have never learned to pop a bull whip, it can be an equalizer, no matter how macho or jock you are. So I challenged the jock to try it. Not knowing any better, he tried and proceeded to put whelps on his body each time he messed up. Now being a proper host, I offered to teach him. This whip-popping teaching process finally winds up with the teacher standing behind and very close to the student—a perfect place to be if you want to push someone into a swimming pool. With one hand holding my whip I used my other hand to gently shove his jock butt into the pool. I taught him about the difference between well-built jocks and older, smarter, and more experienced nonjock folks.

This story didn't directly involve our kids, but it is a kid story worth telling. One day, the day of Halloween, a group of us chemical-plant maintenance workers decided to cook some deer chili for the maintenance department to eat the next day at noon. We gathered at one of the guy's houses and proceeded to cut up the fixings, meat, onions, etc. Out in the garage, we set up a big iron pot and got a fire started under it. Soon, we were all cooking chili and drinking beer in the garage. And drinking beer and drinking beer. As it got dark, we started to notice a lot of kids walking down the street out in front of the garage. Finally, someone realized it was Halloween night. Well okay, but we didn't have a plan for that, and we didn't have anything for the kids. We tried to ignore them, thinking they would just pass us up but that did not work on all of them. They put me in charge of handling the situation. Next bunch came up and I invited them into the garage and offered each of them a ladle of hot chili to put in their bag. If we had had YouTube back then, the looks on those kids faces would have went viral. Thankfully, the parents stayed out on the road so they couldn't see what I was doing; else, I might not be alive or free today. I suppose also, lucky for me, that the parents didn't believe what the kids told them. True story, it really happened.

Our kids invented a saying that survives in our family today. It goes like this: "We just took out the important pieces". Somewhere around when the kids were about eleven years old, my wife accused the boys of doing just that to their sister. Some who knew our daughter would wonder, just maybe that's true. This infamous saying came from an incident involving the boys' collection of used bicycles. Unbeknownst to me, the boys started to collect throwaway bicycles from the alleys on their way walking home from school each day. I saw them messing with these bicycles from time to time and thought nothing of it till one day when I went up into our attic; the attic was neck-deep in bicycles. When I saw them next, I gave orders to get the bicycles out of the attic before the entire house collapsed. Soon, I began to notice bicycle parts in the trash and assumed all was going well. Next trip up in the attic, I found many coffee cans full of small bicycle parts. There were coffee cans full of nuts, screws, spokes, spoke ends, ball bearings, ball bearing races, etc. They had disassembled the bicycles down to the least factory parts level. I asked what the heck that was that all about and their answer was "We just took out the important pieces".

This next story is a little off-color so you might want to skip it. It, however, truly did happen just as I'm about to tell it. During my early work career, as a new branch manager, I opened a new office for the consulting firm that had just bought out my very small company. I rented a building and as a way to make more money, I hired my young, very young kids and my wife to do the janitor work. This new business venture was a learning experience for me as well as our kids. One of the learning experiences for the kids was, for the first time in their lives, to see a person of nonwhite color with eyes that were not like theirs. They had never seen a foreigner. One of my new employees was just such a fellow and his name will be, for this story, Lee, a shortened version of his real name. I had to take advantage of this and I did. One night, just before the kids showed up for janitor service, I dumped some leftover ice cubes in the men's toilet. The ice cubes, after a few minutes, got oblong, rounded, and opaque white. They looked very interesting floating in the toilet. As soon as the kids came in to the office to start the cleanup, I asked them, and my wife as well, if they had ever seen a foreigner's turd? I told them that Lee (they knew Lee) had not flushed the toilet the last time he went, so go have a look. My wife, rightfully so, thought I was nuts, but couldn't help but look when the kids did. I'd give anything to know just what they thought when they saw those oblong, rounded, opaque white things in the men's toilet. Before the afternoon was over, I found out what my wife thought of me. Don't know how many years it was before our kids learned that foreign turds are not foreign looking, assuming they did. I never told them so. Not sure my daughter knows the truth today, and I'm not about to ask.

These were just a few of my fun kid stories. I'm sure that if you raised kids, you have a few of your own. Don't forget the funny ones. You need memory and talent to tell jokes; not so for funny kid stories. Tell the fun stories. Your friends (audience) can't be thinking about their troubles while listing to a funny kid story. Give 'em a break; put a smile on their faces.

# Petrochemicals: What, Why and How?

This story was originally published as a five-part series in a local newspaper near where I live. All the names have been omitted since they contribute nothing to the general readership. It's not exactly a funny or old-history story, but it does convey an important message as most stories do, so maybe it belongs here. I hope it works for you.

You're in Walmart shopping. You're looking at lots of different products. To some of us, it's like being a kid in a candy store. So many good things, you can't decide what to buy next. There's shoes, clothes, food, electronic stuff, do-it-yourself stuff, appliances, drugs, furniture, garden stuff, and the list goes on and on. Of course, we know where they come from; somebody or some company grows them or makes them. That's a rather simple answer but one that we generally accept. Who needs to know more and what difference does it make? Would you ever guess that if petrochemical complexes didn't exist, Walmart would not exist? Walmart probably does not sell a single product that doesn't depend, in some way, on oil or gas processed by the petrochemical industry.

When I first decided to write this story, I asked several major petrochemical companies (this general term *petrochemical* here includes refineries) for a list of all the chemicals or energy products (fuels) they make and what retail products they could be found in. Initially, I intended to list all of them with their retail connections. The list, however, was much longer than I anticipated; the retail product list was basically everything Walmart sells and more. So instead I'll just point out a few examples and try, as best as I can as a mechanical engineer, to explain just how a lot of that stuff, tanks, towers, etc., across the fence works to make a Walmart retail product. I might not get the chemical part exactly right (some of it is really complicated), but I think I can get it close to right and describe much of it in a way most folks can understand.

The big dogs in town are the refineries. They get the first shot at the oil and natural gas and then they squeeze as much energy stuff (gasoline, diesel, jet fuel, propane, methane (natural gas), and fuel oil) out of it as they can, about 70 percent of each barrel or barrel equivalent. The leftovers, about 30 percent, are really the cream, the chemicals that get further processed to make Walmart what it is today. A side note here: as you might learn from this story and others, crude oil (petroleum) is so valuable for the chemicals in it that burning oil in automobiles is like burning the furniture in your house to keep warm. We can and will solve this problem someday. The alternative, when we run out, is going back to milking cows, planting corn (all in the backyard), and making clothes out of cotton cow-feed sacks. Been there, done that. Don't be fooled by the news of increased production from fracking shale deposits. Increased production is not the same thing as abundant supply; we still have very little supply as compared to the other oil-rich sources. Let's not simply "drill, baby, drill" and run out of oil before they do. Buying oil now is bad enough; future begging or fighting for it will be a lot worse. I say let's use their oil up first.

Remember I promised to explain how all that works? It all starts with oil and natural gas that comes out of the ground. The oil (forget the gas for now to keep the story simpler) is then collected in small tanks or pumped directly into pipelines for final transport to one of the refineries' very large, round storage tanks. Other sources are from ships that were filled by overseas suppliers. This stuff is like muddy water, so the first thing we want to do is separate the good stuff from the mud by heating it till it boils. Most of the time it is heated with steam (very hot water vapor) because it's safer that way (remember the oil will burn if lit). That's why you see so much steam at refineries. Back to the oil boiling; when you boil water on your stove at home, most of the vaporized water is wasted in the air while some will condense (go back to a liquid) on a cold glass. This similar vapor produced by boiling oil is the part we want—the gasoline, propane, etc. and chemicals. So we contain it in tall tanks called towers and condense most it with heat exchangers (devices similar to your AC unit beside your house) back to liquids. The vertical location on the tower determines what product is produced, the bottom is mud or tar, and the top may be propane, with gasoline somewhere in the middle. When Henry Ford started making cars (1903), that's all there was to it. We still do the main part that way, but the chemical engineers have found better ways to get more of the desired product out at lower cost. So other complicated processes are also part of this otherwise simple operation. The term *cat-cracking* we often hear is one of those special, complicated processes.

Let's pause here and consider just how simple and unique crude oil is. We generally refer to oil and oil-derived chemicals as hydrocarbons. This is because crude oil is simply a mixture of combinations of hydrogen and carbon, two very basic elements. These elements occur naturally combined in many ways, each combination being a different chemical with its own unique properties. Chemical engineers can manipulate these combinations in various ways to produce desired products. This manipulation process is what petrochemical plants do.

As an example of one of the more complicated manipulations to get more and better chemicals, let's start with a chemical called paraxylene. Let's say paraxylene is the house we want to build. Naturally occurring in the crude oil after the refineries get most of the gasoline out is a by-product we call mixed xylenes, the materials we will need to build the house. To convert the mixed xylenes into paraxylene, we need a big pot (tank) called a reactor, tools to make the conversion (catalyst), and probably some heat. Kind of like the beer-making process where the sugar is converted to alcohol using yeast (the tools). The yeast or the catalyst gets worn a little but do not end up in the product and can be used again. Next step now is to separate the paraxylene from the other unwanted, by-product chemicals. Since its boiling point is very close to the other unwanted chemicals, it can't be separated or purified by distillation (the way they make whiskey) without several towers (stills), each being about a half a mile tall. Lucky for us, it has a very different freezing point. So we can just freeze it in giant ice-cream freezers. The frozen stuff (paraxylene) is then separated by centrifuging (remember high school chemistry) then remelted. Next step is a pipeline trip to the docks and loading on a barge or ship. One of many places it may go to is to another chemical plant where they use it to make PTA. The chemical processes get complicated here, so I'll end this story with this. PTA goes on to make polyester fibers, which when added to natural fibers makes clothes perma-press. No paraxylene, no perma-press. How about it, ladies, want to go back to before paraxylene? Another major use is the plastic bottles that contain the bottled water we buy.

Some petrochemical plants are very specialized and produce a surprising number of special chemicals. The list of their products is amazing in its length and its unpronounceable names. Their products wind up in everything from paint to adhesives to detergents to beer to ink and, most surprising to me, pharmaceuticals. I guess you could make beer without using their products but, as I recall from personal experience, it might not be as good.

The bottom line for petrochemical communities is this: start with a lot of smart and hardworking people, then take some oil out of the ground, use pipes and tanks to separate the main energy parts, and then use chemistry to change the rest into thousands of products for Walmart to sell. The petrochemical process is as natural as farming and milking cows. The smart, hardworking folks work just like farmers for the same reasons. When you think about it, the men and women that work twenty-four hours a day in the plants are kind of like cooks. Not surprising to me to see them at cooking contests (barbecue, chili, gumbo, etc.) on weekends. They are doing the same thing. They are using fire, gas, pots, tanks, and chemicals to make good stuff. Farmers and cooks work as safe as they can because they don't want to hurt themselves, their neighbors, or the land. Petrochemical employees and plant owners likewise do not want to hurt themselves, their neighbors, or the land.

In the nineteenth century (1800s) before the petrochemicals as we know them today, our life expectancy, at best, was about forty to fifty years (didn't need social security—no one lived long enough to collect it). Today's life expectancy is—well, I'm old and looking forward to one hundred. By now, you know I am a fan of petrochemicals (I believe them to be responsible for my extra, safe, and healthy years with more to come) and our healthy, prosperous, and safe way of life in petrochemical communities. I have lived long enough and worked long enough in the industry to have seen many changes for the better. Every day our petrochemical owners and workers find better, safer, and more economical ways to make products that afford us our outstanding standard of living and long life. Lest we forget, remember the used-to-be dominant (only American) auto industry, the used-to-be dominant steel industry, and the used-to-be dominant garment industry. Let's not let that happen again and have our kids write about the used-to-be dominant petrochemical industry.

One final story. I remember a day back in Nederland, Texas (when Bum Phillips was there, head coach, not student—I'm not that old), as a young teenager, complaining to the City Auto Parts store clerk that the price of their spark plugs was ridiculously high. His response was simply, Son you always have the option to make your own. So I say to those folks that seem to think we are doing it all wrong: Don't use our gasoline or paraxylene; *exercise your option to make your own.*

Seriously, I hope this cow-milking-farmer way (I really did that as a kid) of informing you as to what's going on behind those fences has helped a little. The highly trained and experienced plant workers are doing very important jobs. Their jobs are not the safest in the world but they have to be done. Those jobs, however, are far safer than our everyday home-life experiences that involve driving cars, drinking alcohol, tobacco smoking/dipping, and dodging bullets. We are all infinitely safer and better off with petrochemicals and petrochemical jobs than without them. Remember there are no 100-percent-safe jobs, not even kindergarten teaching; but jobs must be done. All working people deserve our thanks, support, and help in maintaining their places of employment.

Still, it's right and fair to demand safe and environment-friendly operations (and safe jobs) from all of our industry and employers, including petrochemicals, but let's do it in a way that supports our livelihood and maintains our high standard of living. It doesn't have to be and shouldn't be a fight. It's not us or them, it's *us*

# Polarization Invisibility

Now this is going to be rather technical, but if you read it slowly, I believe you will be able to get it. To start with, polarization has to do with seeing light as two perpendicular waves. I told you it might be a little tough. Perpendicular means like one is maybe horizontal and the other is vertical. Still tough, isn't it? Try this. Picture a cross. The vertical post is the vertical part and the cross piece is the horizontal part. So picture the light as being made up of horizontal parts and vertical parts. Glass can be made such that it will transmit only one of these two parts. It's called a polarized lens when it does that. Now, if you use two polarized lens to view something, when you turn the lenses a certain way, the image will disappear. Now that's a neat trick that we are going to discuss here.

This story has to do with military secrets, so secret that the fact that I worked on it is so secret that it is unknown to everybody. Even I am barely aware of my role in this. Being at that secret level, there are no records of who or what, so I can't be accused of revealing secrets that don't even exist. So here's the story.

At the beginning of the Iraq War, we put together a secret plan to make part of our war efforts invisible to Iraqi soldiers. The way this was supposed to work was that we would appear to lose truckloads of equipment in the war zone. These trucks at first contained polarized sunglasses that looked like the ones Saddam wore. We assumed correctly that the soldiers would want to look like Saddam so they would all wear the sunglasses; and they did. Next step was to lose truckloads of high-class sexy-looking polarized rearview mirrors, thinking that they would install them on all their vehicles. The idea being that the combination of the polarized sunglasses and the specially oriented and treated rearview mirrors would make moving objects behind them, as seen in the rearview mirror, invisible. They could not see us sneaking up from behind their vehicles. A nine-year-old genius came up with this idea. Unfortunately, the war didn't last long enough to test the idea very well. The part about only moving objects being invisible was never proven to work.

As it turned out, this was a big mistake that caused us real problems after the war. You see, with every male in Iraq wearing the polarized Saddam-looking sunglasses, we couldn't tell who was Saddam and who wasn't; seems he was everywhere.

Having not been paid for my part in this grand plan (it was so secret they didn't know where to send my checks), I figured it was okay for me to use the science to my benefit if I could; and so I did and here is how.

Remember CB radios? I do, and I remember them being a really fun part of my life. We used to go camping nearly every weekend, and this meant we were driving for about two hours and talking on the CB radio to whomever. To get to where we usually went, we had to go through a single-lane tunnel that had a two-lane bottleneck at the entrance. No problem, as soon as we got close, I would announce a wreck in the left lane, even though there really wasn't one. As we traveled in the left lane, cars kept moving out of our way as they tried to get into the right lane that they thought was clear. Worked every weekend.

Just one of many CB stories, but the polarized invisibility story however goes like this. During our every weekend trip, we had long stretches of country roads where we might see only one car. The others did not exist, or as we would convey, they were invisible. When we saw a car, we would pass it and, (if he was wearing sunglasses) after getting a ways ahead, start talking to the driver on the CB; remember everybody had CB radios. I say *we* because my daughter and I both talked to the poor unsuspecting soul from the same car on the same radio. We talked as if we were in two cars—one in front of him that he could see and one behind him that he could not see. At first he would strain his eyes and doubt and wonder why he could not see the car behind him that obviously could see him. After messing with his mind for a while, I would tell him about the Iraq grand plan. As he began to understand it, I suggested that his car might have these leftover polarized rearview mirrors installed. During the Iraq War, all auto companies made these special rearview mirrors. I suggested that he either change his sunglasses to nonpolarized lenses or take his car back to the dealership to have all the rearview mirrors changed back to the standard glass. More than one bought this story, believing that some moving cars behind them would be invisible. How they assumed only some would be invisible instead of all, I don't know. I wish I could have followed one of them to a dealership and listened to him tell this story. This nearly really did happen; this is a nearly true story. The CB part is definitely true; I swear it.

Weren't thinking about your problems while you read this bit of wit, were you?

# Rainbow Bridge

Author unknown, wish it was me.

Just this side of heaven is a place called Rainbow Bridge.

When a pet animal dies that has been especially close to someone here, that pet goes to Rainbow Bridge. There are meadows and hills for all of our special friends so they can run and play together. There is plenty of food and water and sunshine, and our friends are warm and comfortable. All the pet animals that had been ill and old are restored to health and vigor; those who were hurt or maimed are made whole and strong again, just as we remember them in our dreams of days and times gone by.

The animals are happy and content except for one small thing: they miss someone very special to them, who had to be left behind.

They all run and play together, but the day comes when one suddenly stops and looks into the distance. The bright eyes are intent; the eager body quivers. Suddenly he/she begins to break away from the group, flying over the green grass, his/her legs carrying him/her faster and faster. You have been spotted, and when you and your special friend finally meet, you cling together in joyous reunion, never to be parted again. The happy kisses rain upon your face, your hands again caress the beloved head, and you look once more into the trusting eyes of your pet, so long gone from your life but never absent from your heart.

Then you cross the Rainbow Bridge together.

# Report on Hell

If you can't take the heat, this might be your fire. You might want to skip this story if you are touchy about your religious beliefs. Remember I warned you.

This is a kind of thought-provoking rambling about hell. I'm not saying it's so, only that one might imagine that just maybe.

Imagine for a short while that I just showed up at the entrance to hell. Probably will be one of those "self machines" with the first question "Select a language". I'm sure that hell would not pass up an opportunity to make me mad. I hate those machines. Now understand; I'm not at the gates of hell because I died and was sent there. Actually, by special permission (can't say from whom), I'm there as a reporter to write a story about how things are going in hell. A hell of an assignment, wouldn't you say? Unlike heaven where God is busy, the devil is at the door to greet me in person. The interview goes like this:

Me: I'm here to see the devil.
Devil: If you mean Lucifer or Satan, then that's me.
Me: So you are the devil or, as you say, Satan?
Devil: Yes.
Me: Well, I was expecting a greeter but if it's your policy to greet in person, so be it.
Devil: It is. So what can I do for you as I see you are here only temporarily?
Me: I just want to see how things are going down here and report back upstairs.
Devil: Okay, first question?
Me: How about showing me around? I want to see how big this place is.
Devil: Don't worry about that, it's big enough.

Me: I understand that you are actually an angel that went bad. Any truth to that?

Devil: That's about it. I had a really bad day with God and so here I am taking care of God's problems.

Me: By the way, since I can't get a technical answer from God and you have obviously talked to God, do you know how old God is?

Devil: Actually, I don't know. I can only tell you what God used to say all the time. I'm older than dirt.

Me: That's not much help; that's about the same as a father saying he is older than his kids.

Devil: Do you realize you are wasting my time? Do you want to know anything important?

Me: Well, yes. How many people are down here now?

Devil: I would rather not answer that question.

Me: It's my main question and a pretty simple one at that. What's the problem?

Devil: By the way, who sent you down here and why is that question so important?

Me: I would rather not answer that question.

Devil: Do you realize who you are getting smart-alecky with?

Me: Well, with a free pass back upside, I'm really not too scared of you.

Devil: Next question.

Me: How do you handle cremations? I mean after a cremation, what are you going to burn forever?

Devil: I don't know, it never came up yet.

Me: You mean that so far, everyone who was cremated went to heaven?

Devil: No, I didn't say that.

Me: Well, how else do you account for your answer?

Devil: Well, since you are going to find out anyway, the answer to your main question is one and it wasn't a cremation.

Me: What do you mean one? What question are you answering?

Devil: You asked how many people are down here and the answer is one if you count me.

Me: You mean there is no one down here burning forever?

Devil: That's right. God has not let a single soul get here yet.

Me: That's hard to believe. What happened to what the preachers been saying? They been lying or what?

Devil: The problem is I didn't read the fine print when I made the deal with God to run this place. It's God's stuff about everybody being God's children and God, just like you, will never send a child down here.

Me: Ordinarily, I'd say I was sorry for you about that, but in this case I'm not sorry at all.

Devil: Do you talk to God? Do you think you could get God to change the deal just a little so I can have a reason to be here? Heck, I have never even tried to start the fires down here. I'm seriously lonely and bored.

Me: You want me to ask God to send people down here to burn forever just because you are lonely and bored? Are you nuts?

Devil: How about this. For those who don't want to sing in heaven, send them down here and we will drink beer and barbecue. Forget that burning forever stuff. I never really bought into that deal myself.

Me: Now you are getting me interested. How about this. When they write the next testament of the Bible, ask God to rewrite the hell part. Change the name of this place and give everyone a choice: singing up in heaven or outdoor cooking down here. And of course, everyone can travel up or down anytime at their pleasure.

Devil: Hey, I like that idea. But I'll have to get seriously right with God before I even ask for something like that.

Me: Do you realize that I can't see you? I have no idea what you look like.

Devil: Can't see ghosts, souls, or angels either, can you?

Me: No.

Devil: I can't tell you why, but I will tell you this: I don't have horns, I don't have a tail, and I'm not red.

Me: Well, I guess I have to get to the end of this, so let me see if I have it right. No one is here burning forever, you don't like your job, and you think we ought to convert this place to a heaven alternative for the nonsinging rednecks, Cajuns, and backsliders.

Devil: Sounds good to me.

About this time I woke up and realized that it was the Bush Beans that had been tormenting me all night and making me dream. And then I remembered that I had not had any Bush Beans in over a week. So was it a dream or?

# Sewer Safari

My first real job after high school and the Marine Corps was with the Texas Highway Department. I'll try to protect the innocent, if any, by not naming the location or any individuals involved. Let's say the town was X and the only other actor was DA-2 for dumb-ass number 2. I was DA-1.

We were building a new road through an old rice field with drainage canals everywhere. Naturally, there were snakes, rabbits, coons, opossums, rats, mice, etc. everywhere and we had heard stories of alligators but hadn't actually seen an alligator. Highway construction requires drainage, and in this case, long runs of concrete pipe starting out at about twenty-four inches in diameter, increasing in pipe size and finally to large concrete square-box tubes. As you got closer to the drainage canal, the collection pipe system naturally got larger. Now, as the construction progressed, all this system got buried so from the ground there was no way to know just what shape it was in after the final burial. Kind of like a grave the day after a funeral. But this is not a funeral; this is a Texas Highway Department project, so we must know it is in compliance with the construction specifications. We need to know that it is in good shape, not broke, no holes or leaks, not full of dirt, and capable of doing its intended job. It must be inspected.

Now came DA-1 and DA-2. Both of us were lowest on the totem pole of eligible inspectors. Sure we would get inside the pipe system and check it out from the inside. Remembering the snakes and alligator stories, we armed ourselves with three-foot long sticks, two flashlights, and my .22 caliber revolver pistol with nine rounds of ammunition, just in case. The system was about a half-mile long with square inlet boxes about every three hundred feet. These boxes had cast-iron grates on top to allow the water in and personal in for maintenance and inspections. Now think about this. If I fire a bullet down

## True Story, I Swear It - Maybe

a round pipe and it hits the solid wall of one of the inlet boxes, might not it come back down the pipe and hit DA-1 or DA-2? So using the pistol for protection might not be such a good idea; but we brought it anyway.

We got in the pipe system where it was about forty-eight inches in diameter. We looked back with our flashlights to see that the smaller sections appeared to be okay. As we progressed through the pipes, they got larger and we started noticing that we were wading through water. And then the fun started. There in front of us was a big snake. The pipe wasn't big enough for us to walk around the snake, so it was him or us. We solved the problem with one of the sticks. Then it happened again and again. Finally, the water got so deep that the snakes were swimming and we couldn't kill them with the sticks. It's time to get out of here and forget this stupid adventure job.

So at the next box we came to, we climbed the ladder and tried to raise the iron grate so we could get out. It wouldn't budge; it was stuck with splashed concrete from the box construction. We hollered help but no one could hear us. So we thought about going back but remembered some of the snakes we whacked with a stick didn't die, were hidden in the muddy water, and mad as hell. No we can't go back. So let's go to the next box and try to get out there. More snakes and we still can't get out. Now we had a problem. Trying to kill a swimming snake with a stick wasn't working. The snakes would disappear under the muddy water. Not good because we had to make our way by the snake not knowing where it was or what it might do. We had rubber boots but these were big snakes. It's time for the pistol and taking a chance we might shoot ourselves with the ricochet bullets. I was a pretty good shot even with the short-barrel .22 so I thought we would be safe so long as I hit the snake.

Next snake is instantly dead with a .22 hole in its head. Things are looking up so we moved on. Finally we got into the big box which was about eight foot square with water about two feet deep. We could actually see light at the end of the box but were not out yet. The box was big enough now so we could actually walk by smaller snakes without risking shooting with the pistol. And besides, we were down to one bullet left.

And then it got real scary again. Just ahead of us was two eyes about six inches apart on top of the water looking right at us—an alligator which must be about six or eight feet long. We can't walk by that sucker. To make this long story a little shorter, it was just shoot and hope. I shot that dude right between the eyes and it didn't even move. We still had to get by him one way or the other though. We got close and used one of the sticks to try to lift him out of the water. When I touched him, he came alive and ate me, and that's why I can't finish this story.

A final note from DA-2: he's lying. We tried to raise that gator to make sure it was dead and to see how big it was. Everywhere we stuck the stick nothing came up. So we stuck it right under its head and raised it up. It wasn't an alligator; it was a big and I mean *big* bullfrog dead with a .22-sized hole in its head. I took it home and ate it.

There was another half-mile pipe system on the same job going the other direction. To my knowledge, it has never been inspected. I sure as heck wasn't going to do it and neither was DA-1 or DA-2. I forgot who's telling this story.

I later moved up in the ranks and got an inside job, and that's another story.

# Smart First Grader

Contributed by secret author

Have you ever watched the show *Are You Smarter than a 5th Grader?* If you have, then you will understand that sometimes kids can be smarter than adults. I'm a little embarrassed to say that I am the adult who was outsmarted by a little first grader. In order to protect the identity of this student and myself, names have been changed in this story. Of course, I am the teacher of this first grader, so the protection of my name is most important because my job depends on it. Who wants a teacher who admits she was outsmarted by a first grader? Well, I have been teaching for twenty years now, and my students have taught me more than any college class.

Several years ago, I had the pleasure of learning from a little seven-year-old boy named Jimmy. Jimmy was a student who had an outgoing personality and lots of energy that often got him in trouble with many teachers and the principal. His mom and I were on a first-name basis. We had daily telephone conversations about how Jimmy could express himself in a more positive manner. One day I was not feeling well, so I called in for a substitute teacher to take my place and I took the day off to rest. After returning to school the next day, I arrived early only to have the principal call me into her office. I knew something had to have happened while I was out. She began to tell me about an incident involving Jimmy and the substitute teacher. Jimmy had fallen down in the classroom and hurt his leg. Apparently, he was in such pain that he appeared to be dead. All the students and the substitute were very concerned, so the nurse and the principal were informed of the emergency and rushed to my room. As the nurse assessed the situation, little Jimmy rose from the dead and announced that he thought he would be okay. Of course, little Jimmy was removed from the room for the day so he could be watched as he recovered. Like always, little Jimmy was just seeking attention, and he was not really hurt at all.

Well, after hearing little Jimmy's attention-seeking story, I thought of a way to give him the attention he so deserved. When lunchtime arrived, I told the class I would be eating lunch with them because the substitute teacher had left a note saying the class was very well-behaved. The students were excited to have me as their lunch partner, especially little Jimmy. During lunch, I made sure I sat right next to him. Jimmy and I made small talk for several minutes. I asked him if his mom was coming for her parent conference. He stated that yes, she would be coming because she really wanted to meet me. I said great, because I really want to meet her too. Jimmy was so excited that I wanted to meet his mom. After giving this a little thought, he then asked, "Why do you want to meet her?" I informed him that I knew about his playing-dead incident and that I thought his mom should know about it as well. He sat there for a while not saying a word, and then he asked, "What day is parent conferences?" I replied, "Tomorrow night at seven o'clock." He said, "Oh, she will not be able to come that night because she is getting married." I gave little Jimmy too much information and he used it wisely. I don't know what he told his mom, but she never made it to his parent conference. I do know that she was already married, so Jimmy's excuse was not what kept her from the conference.

Little Jimmy's mom is now the principal's secretary, so he is getting all the attention he so much wanted. Jimmy is the student I will always remember because he taught me to see humor in all situations.

Comment from this book's author, Harvey Cappel

I need to locate Jimmy. It sounds to me like that little dude's brain is a gold mine of tall tales. I might just hire him as a consultant and contributing author for my next book. By the way, if you want to know more about this story's female secret author, read "Our Kids' Stories" in this book.

# Smokey-Water Myth Busted

Smokey Yunick was a great mechanic and a smart fellow. Unlike me, he has a clanlike following that believes just about everything he says. I have to prove everything I say. But like me, from time to time what is said can be misinterpreted such that the story as retold is not true.

In the case I'm about to discuss, I'm going to give Smokey the benefit of the doubt and assume that he has been misquoted and misunderstood and that he, like me, really knows that:

> *"Running water through a radiator faster will not cause a water-cooled internal combustion engine to run hotter."*

Actually, there is a minor case where this will actually happen. Take an old car that has a severely damaged radiator that's causing the engine to run hot. First thought for an easy cheap fix is to remove the thermostat. What can happen in this case, and often does, is that the increased water flow through the damaged radiator does very little to transfer any more heat but does increase the engine load by having the water pump work harder to pump more water. More engine load, more heat. More engine heat; higher engine temperature.

The misunderstanding about this myth comes from confusing temperature with heat. Yes, if you increase the flow of water through a radiator, the outlet temperature will rise, indicating that the water did not have enough time in the radiator to cool. The rise in temperature is true; it does happen. This does not however translate into the wrong conclusion that the radiator is not cooling more water. It is, and this **extra** water (even though it is slightly hotter) will in fact take more heat away from the motor and cause it to run cooler. You just can't say it or think it any other way.

Let's look at an example of what is happening with the radiator.

Consider the following:

>Inlet temperature: 200°F
>Outlet temperature: 150°F
>Ambient air temperature: 90°F

The heat transfer from the radiator to the air will be proportional to the fan flow rate times the difference in average radiator temperature and ambient air (200-150)/2 - (90) = 85. So the 85 degrees is the driving force taking heat away from the radiator by the fan. The heat transfer is going from the hot radiator to the cooler air.

Now let's increase the water flow rate so that the outlet temperature rises because the water has less time in the radiator to cool.

>Inlet temperature: 200°F
>Outlet temperature: 190°F
>Ambient temperature: 90°F

The heat transfer rate from the radiator to the air will again be proportional to the same fan flow rate times the difference in average radiator temperature and ambient air, (200+190)/2 - (90) = 105. So the 105 degrees is the driving force taking heat away from the radiator by the fan.

Obviously, the radiator is operating more efficiently because of the higher temperature and is in fact taking more heat away from the circulating water. Since this is a closed system (forget the motor heat transfer directly to air) the heat transfer in the system must balance. If the radiator is taking heat out of the system then that heat must come from the motor. If we take heat away from the motor then its temperature must change; it must go down. This seems a little counterintuitive I know. It would seem that the cooler motor could not be transferring more heat away into the radiator water. Look at it this way. Consider that instead of water we had little men with buckets taking heat away from the motor. The sizes of the buckets are set by the temperature difference between the motor and the radiator water. When we increase the flow rate of water making the motor cool down the buckets get smaller. But the way we did it was to increase the number of men hauling the buckets. More men hauling small buckets can sometimes do a better job than fewer men hauling big buckets.

But you knew all along that putting *more* water on a fire could not possibly cause the fire to get hotter, didn't you?

And finally if you ever actually see little men in your water please call me. I can always use new material for true stories.

# Snake Stories

Now if you have an ophidiophobia, better pass on these stories. I've never been that much afraid of snakes but I do jump when surprised by one, the same as almost everybody does. However, not being afraid and having three sons that are also not afraid, one can have some fun snake experiences, as follows:

One day a long time ago, my school buddy and I were doing what we called hunting in a large field behind my house—actually, it was a dairy farm. Through the property ran an old interurban right-of-way and a drainage canal. We could always find birds (quail and doves) to shoot and occasionally an unlucky rabbit. On this day, we were walking along the canal when we spotted a long snake at the edge of the water. It was about six feet long and had two tails and no head. Needless to say, this got our attention. We knew about snakes but had never seen anything like this. Now as you might imagine, this snake with two tails and no head was not very good at crawling in any direction, so it didn't go anywhere while we looked at it and poked it. As we got braver and got closer looks, we finally figured out the problem. It was two snakes; one eating the other. Now I don't recall what we did at this point but I can say it was a sight to see and a neat story to tell.

This same buddy mentioned above was kind of macho and somewhat larger than me. He played football and sometimes protected me from bullies but he was afraid of snakes. One day I, took him to work with me. I worked after school every day at a drive-in theater. He would just sit in the car watch the movies, and after work we would watch what was left of the movies together and go home. This day, however, before the movies started, I was walking up to my car to tell him something when I saw a grass snake crawling on the ground in front of me. I bet you can guess most of the story from here.

You're right; I picked up the snake as I walked up to my car where he was sitting with the window rolled down. I dropped that snake in his lap. I know his first thought was to run but he couldn't because he was in the car. Second thought, which he did, was to just grab the snake and chunk it out of the car. He grabbed the snake about mid length and immediately the snake turned half its body around and bit him on the back of his hand. I guess he thought he was going to die then. He didn't die, but he came close to killing me. It was worth it though; I'd do it again. If you see me coming from behind, better check out what's in my hands.

There must be something wrong with me to tell these snake stories and think they are funny, but you are reading it, so. This next one was the result of a having a lot of United Stated marines all gathered in a field with nothing to do—not a good idea. We were on an advanced infantry training exercise learning how to shoot flamethrowers. The site was on Camp Pendleton in the mountains near a canal. With only four training flamethrowers, several hundred of us had nothing to do for long periods of time, waiting our turn.

That's where this bunch of Cajuns (Coonasses to us in the South) came into the story. By the way, Coonass is not necessarily a derogatory term to most Cajuns especially if it is used appropriately. Anyway, these Cajuns were exploring the canal looking for crawfish, I guess, when they instead found a bunch of very large dead snakes. Did I say they killed them? In any case, they started bringing them up the hill to show us and then it happened. Several marines were lying around on the ground asleep. You guessed it. They put the dead snakes on the sleeping marines then woke them up. First, the entertainment was funny, and then it changed to extemporaneous hand-to-hand combat—not training but the real thing. Now I was raised part Cajun and I love jokes and I am not afraid of snakes. However, if you were a marine there that day, I didn't do it, don't come looking for me. I just watched the show.

Last snake story, I promise. During our early marriage years when our kids were growing up, we camped out a lot. One night after a late camp set up in the rain, I picked up a pile of brush to make a fire and out of it came a big snake headed for my wife. Within two hours we were home; camping trip over. That's not the story, however. The story is we again were camping in Louisiana under the bridge at Lake Charles. It was early spring and the days were getting warm. Our kids, three boys and a girl were exploring and happened upon a bunch of garter snakes (long and green) coming out of hibernation. They, of course, caught about twenty or thirty of them in paper grocery bags. Needless to say, my wife did not approve, but the kids and I kept them anyway, out of her sight.

Next day, we were planning to leave and had to make a decision about how we were going to get the snakes home. Picture this: the early morning was cool so we had a big campfire. The campsite was like a circle with every camper backed up to the central circle where the big community fire was. It was late in the morning so the fire was all but out but still hot. This is important for you to know especially if you think snakes should not be harmed. Before I finish the story I am telling you, we did not seriously harm any snakes. My wife suspected what me and the kids were about and asked about the snakes in the bags. I said we could haul them in the pop-up camper with the bags secured with no problem. She said—and grabbed both bags and threw them into the fire. The bags were open and the ground was hot and the snakes came out very fast in all directions. Next were the campers—they scattered also in every direction running from the hot and excited snakes. What did I do? Broke camp at record speed and got the hell out of there before they found out where the snakes came from. The lesson learned by me and the kids? Don't even think about mixing snakes and my wife.

# Steve's Garage

I grew up in a small town back when cars were cars and everybody could work on them. This, however, didn't mean that we didn't have car-repair businesses or, as we called, them garages. From an early age, my daddy taught me how to fix things, especially cars, so I naturally liked to be around cars and garages where they worked on and fixed cars. I guess the term naturally isn't right for everyone, but it was for me. In any case, I spent a lot of my early years hanging out at a place called Steve's Garage (not the real name). Now the owner, Steve, and his partner were fun guys and liked to drink as did many folks back then. Unfortunately for all of us back then, drinking and smoking was the norm, and if you didn't do both, something was wrong with you. In fact, the more you could drink and the drunker you could get, the more popular you were. Sad state of affairs, but that's the way it was then. It was fun but at a high price, and much higher today.

So a full day at Steve's garage was to witness a lot of drinking and some crazy things going on. Enough about the drinking except that it probably was a factor in a lot of the crazy happenings.

Once upon a time:

You probably are not aware of this, but shotgun shells will explode in a fire without shooting like out of a shotgun. The explosion is more like a firecracker in gravel—a lot of noise and some lead shot flying around rather slowly as compared to being shot out the barrel of a shotgun; scary but not too dangerous. In the winter time when they had radiant gas heaters on in the garage, it wasn't uncommon for one of them fools to lay a shotgun shell on the stove near the flame. They would then find a place on the other end of the shop to work and just let things happen. Scared the heck out of us unsuspecting souls.

One day, I came into the shop as I often did, looked around to see what was going on, and since it was rather cold, I backed up to one of the stoves to get warm. As I stood there getting warm, all of a sudden I realized that the six or eight people I had seen when I walked in had suddenly disappeared; I was in the shop all alone. This wasn't my first rodeo, so real quick I thought something is not right here. I then turned around to look at the stove behind me to see five shotgun shells each backed up to the fire. Naturally, I took off for cover, running into the men's restroom where I found the eight missing folks, one of whom had planted the shotgun shells. About that time, they started exploding and the laughing started and I learned a valuable lesson. Watch them drinking fools and when things don't look right, they aint.

The two partners in the garage were hunters and liked guns of all kinds. They kept a couple of pistols in the garage and brought them out often. One was what we called a German Luger, a rather large-caliber pistol, obviously a dangerous gun. Shooting the pistols in the garage (in town) was common and it would usually bring the local police. Steve's' story was yeah we heard it too, hope you catch that fool. Next day, same thing, same story. I suspect the police knew the truth but what the heck, no one died, so what.

This next trick was their favorite and it wasn't until many years later did I guess how they did it. Late in the afternoon near closing time, when the drinking was taking its toll, Steve would get his partner to stand near the back door of the garage with a cigarette in his mouth. Then Steve pulls out the German Luger, loads it, and proceeds to aim it at his partner near the back of the garage. His partner's position was such that if Steve hit the cigarette then the bullet would lodge in the door frame. If he missed four inches to the right, the bullet would go out the back door and down the road till it hit something or run out of energy and hit the ground. If he missed four inches to the left, he would need a new partner. I saw them do this many times, always hitting the cigarette and breaking it in half. How they broke the cigarette in half, I still don't know but I'd bet my soul that the German Luger was firing blanks. Some of the days when I saw this happen; Steve couldn't hit his own pants pocket with his own hand let alone shoot a pistol straight. It, however, was a show to see.

Another favorite of theirs was to get an acetylene torch burning just right and put it out by rubbing the tip on a wood block. The gas coming out was a very explosive mixture of oxygen and acetylene. The idea now was to use this gas to inflate a large balloon. Next step was to tie a long rag onto the balloon, soak the rag in kerosene, hang the project in a tree, light the rag, and run like hell. Unless you have seen this trick, you can't imagine the sound when the burning rag ignites that balloon full of explosive gas. Now came the police again and the story again: damn we heard it too, hope you catch them fools. Now I hate to say this here because it kind of backfired on me, but *don't do this at home.*

I told my kids this story when the oldest was about twelve the other two boys eleven and ten. Don't do this, I said, you could kill yourself or someone else. We had an acetylene rig in our garage and the boys had my genes—a guaranteed recipe for a fun day or disaster, depending only on luck. One afternoon, my wife and I were having supper when on the garage side of the house we heard an explosion that sounded like one of the petroleum plants had blown up. Within three microseconds, I knew it wasn't a plant explosion. Outside I found one boy standing, looking like he was shell-shocked, and two on the ground. They were not seriously hurt until I got them in the house and seriously abused them. Never tell me or any of my blood kin not to do something.

Just in case you figured out who the partners are in this story, I want you to know that they were not country-bumpkin drunks. They were good friends, good citizens, and both belonged to and supported a very important charity for children.

We can have fun, live close to the edge of the envelope, and still be good folks. I hope.

Now for a final story that probably tells a better truth about the drinking and such. I made a deal with Steve to paint my car, a 1951 Kaiser, if I did all the work of sanding and prepping. The day came for the painting, so I brought the car to the shop early in the morning. I had planned to stay and watch the painting. The morning went by and all Steve did was walk around looking at the car. Then lunch, and more just looking, and now the drinking started. Then more drinking and more just looking. I knew Steve could function after much drinking but I'm wondering about my car, and can he paint drunk? So the day was coming to an end and still no painting, but the drinking—it was doing just fine. Actually I had never seen Steve drink that much. By the way, he was messing with me all day about painting my car, making me nervous about what kind of job I was going to get. He knew I was watching the drinking. Finally just before dark, he started painting. In about an hour, I had a perfect paint job on my car. I didn't know it then, but today I have to believe he was drinking tea all day and having fun watching me worry. Come to think of it, maybe the excess drinking I saw every day was sweet tea. Who knows, and it's too late to ask.

Good days I remember without TV, cell phones, computers, or house keys.

# Toad Suck Fairy Park

Some years ago while traveling in our motor home with another retired couple (no kids), we had just nearly completed our usual, approximately three-week trip. We were leaving Nashville, Tennessee (not more than five minutes on the road) headed south when our lady friend in the other RV came on the CB radio and said let's go to Branson, Missouri, instead of going home. Our response was why not, let's go. Aint retirement good? We quickly had to do a State Farm atlas map search (the best GPS system available at the time, and for some purposes and some people like me, still the best) to see where to turn next to avoid going home. Before we leave the subject of GPS and computer maps—when using them, don't you feel like you are looking at the world through a toilet-paper roll?

Well anyway, we were on our way to Branson, so the next step in the process was to consult our Travel Life directory to see where we can stay tonight. My wife started working on this and came across a park in Conway, Arkansas, called Toad Suck Fairy Park. I looked at her and said yeah, that's funny, but we really need a place to stay tonight so get with the program. She said really, it says that right here. Now I couldn't wait to get on the CB and tell the two following us the news. After much wasted words and laughter, we finally settled on trying to find Toad Suck Fairy Park.

Now finding the place was another story but you are in luck because I'm going to tell it too, right now. The travel guide tells you how to get to your destination, with very detailed instructions like exit at some number and turn right and so on. The last thing you ever want to have is bad information (Travel Life was never wrong till this day) on how to get to a place with a name like Toad Suck Fairy Park, but luck was without us that day and we turned right instead of left. Now for those that don't know, motor homes towing cars don't turn around very easily; in fact it's usually harder to do than an 18-wheeler. Eighteen-wheelers can back up; motor homes towing cars can't. So after the distance traveled, as instructed by the travel guide, we did not see the park. Things were looking bad and it was getting dark, the road was narrow and getting even narrower. Finally, we found a turnaround and now knew we had to ask directions. Remember this was before we had cell phones, and we were going to have to ask someone in person how to get to Toad Suck Fairy Park, keeping in mind that since the travel guide gave us the wrong turn, it's quite possible that Toad Suck Fairy Park too was a mistake and there was no such place. But we had to do something. On the way back to the freeway, we stopped at a small convenience store and I was elected to go in and maybe suffer the embarrassment of asking the dumb question. When I got inside, things got much worse. Remember this was Arkansas and it was cold. In the middle of the store setting in a circle were about seven or eight Indians all playing with bows and arrows—I swear this is the truth. What could I do, I was in too far to go back out, so I boldly asked do you guys or Indians (I didn't say Indians) know how to get to Toad Suck Fairy Park? They did, and they told me we should have turned left when we left the freeway. Two of them took shots at me as I was leaving the store. Just kidding. They were really nice and understood how brave I was to approach them with such a question. I doubt I'd do it again today.

So we found the park and while checking in, I decided that a park with such a name should have a record of Elvis Presley visiting it after everyone, except me, thought he was dead. So I told them my name was Elvis and I was from Memphis, Tennessee. We revisit that park nearly every time we go to Branson, and to this day I am on their computer as Elvis from Memphis, Tennessee. While registering, we noticed a one-legged old man sitting in front of the office—hard to miss him because he was BS-ing more than me while the lady was typing our information and taking our money. After we parked, my traveling friend and I went back to the office to find out the origin of the park name. First off, we could see that it was an old abandoned ferry landing. Believe it or not, that was the first time we actually noticed the spelling of the park name was *ferry* and not *fairy*; kind of took some of the fun out of the situation actually. Anyway, the one-legged old man took it upon himself to answer our question. He said that back in 1831 (that would make him 166 years old on the day of our park visit; this at least helped understand the missing leg; most of us would have been missing much more than one leg) he and some of his friends regularly met on that very spot, much like the Indian meeting we had encountered earlier. One day, with nothing better to do they came up with that name. The meaning, as I understood it, was to describe the men setting around as being like a bunch of toads sucking on I forget what. Think this aint true? Go to Conway, Arkansas, and check it out. At this writing, the one-legged old man should be about 182 years old. Be careful what you ask him.

And finally, one more unbelievable ending to this story. When we got home, my wife related some of this experience to one of her best friends, thinking that no one would believe her. To her surprise, her friend said oh, I know about that park, it's in Conway, Arkansas. Her friend, however, didn't say anything about the Indians or the one-legged old man.

Got a motor home? Go check it out. Nice shaded park on the Arkansas River. The town is okay too.

# Trillion Dollars

Someone once asked me if I know what a trillion dollars is. I know it is a tall stack of green dollar bills. How high, I don't know, but even if I did, it would not be meaningful since I don't measure my income or my debt by how high dollar bills stack. Since this question is a concern about the national debt, that we all owe, I thought it appropriate to see just how much of this debt would be the responsibility of an average single family.

The 2004 census says that the average family in America is 3.18 people. The latest data I can find puts the USA population at just over 316,000,000. Now then, the number of families in the USA would be 316,000,000 divided by 3.18 or equal to roughly 99,000,000 families. I did it this way because families pay taxes, not individuals, especially not children.

So the average family debt for each trillion dollars of national debt will be $1,000,000,000,000 (one trillion) divided by 99,000,000 families or about $10,100. It then is a debt of about $10,100 per family for each trillion dollars of our total national debt.

With the current total USA national debt (year 2013) being about 17 trillion dollars, a per-family debt would then be about $172,000. Not that much different than maybe the average lower-middle-class homeowner's house loan debt. Not a small number, but consider what it represents, in part, as follows. It

1. Provides a very much better defense system than all other countries in the world.
2. Provides the best highway system in the world.

3. Provides a safety net so that no person need starve to death or die from any acute (fixable right now) medical problem.
4. Provides a Medicare and Medicaid system for citizens over sixty-five and the disadvantaged or disabled that is far better than any private insurance in the world.
5. Provides freedom and safety.
6. Provides opportunities for individuals to be all they can be. You can choose to be the richest man in the world, president of the United States, or numerous other choices—yours to freely choose.
7. Provides a safety-net workers retirement system (social security).
8. And the list of USA goods goes on and on.

That's what USA debt is to me. It's high, but it's not the doom and gloom that some will tell you it is. Think of it this way. We each want and need a place to live. The first place and the one everyone will relate to is our house that keeps us comfortable and protects us from pests, both human and insect. For that, we are willing to borrow thousands of dollars and plan for a very long payback. The second consideration is for a place to live that is a safe place for our house. How much is that worth and how do you plan to pay for it? This second place is the United States of America, where we enjoy a better and safer life than any other possible place on earth. That's worth something, and to me it's worth at least the same as my house. So I owe about $172,000 for my house and $172,000 for the privilege of having that house reside in the USA, both on long-term paybacks. This borrowing allows us to have and enjoy today what may not be possible if we lived on a cash basis alone. If we hadn't borrowed to win our wars, our first language today might be German or Japanese. Think about that.

This approved and shared average debt idea, no doubt, will bring on the argument that since not everyone can afford a house with a $172,000 loan, how are those poor people going to be able to pay their share of the $172,000 federal debt. Obviously they can't, and just as obviously, they shouldn't. They are not enjoying an average piece of the USA pie, so they shouldn't have to pay for more than they enjoy. On the other hand, let's say you are fat-catting it to the tune of a $1,000,000 house and enjoying the USA immensely; don't you think you should pay more for your larger share of the USA pie? Taking this idea to its extreme, let's say you owned everything in the USA. You then would be the only one that could pay, and so the fuel bill for all the Air Force's F-16s would have to be paid by you, as well as the light bill for the White House, and on and on. Get the picture? If you are enjoying the USA the most, then you should be paying the most for that enjoyment. Simple as that.

Looking at it from the other perspective, would you ever expect that the privilege of residing in the USA would be free? Roads, F-16s, and safety nets cost something, and someone has to pay for that. Looking around, I can only see you and me, so guess what? You and me have to pay.

As far as this baloney idea that foreign countries are financing our debt, that's another false story. If you had 17 trillion dollars and had the option of keeping it in a shoebox with zero income, investing it in several high-risk countries, or investing it in the USA, what would you do? Investing that much money outside the USA would require investments in several countries. Try naming four or five that you would trust with your trillions of dollars. They all invest money in the USA because we provide the safest and best opportunities for them to make money on their investments. What they (outside and foreign investors) do has nothing to do with any favors of financing our debt.

Okay, the debt is high and we need to pay it and stop spending more than we make or can reasonably expect to pay back. Let's just stop the BS talk and do it.

# Two Funerals

Isn't it a sad state of affairs today that we have to have a funeral to see kinfolks and friends? Were' too busy making money and watching TV to just visit and sit and talk. I remember growing up in a small town, actually before TV, where sitting on the front porch till bedtime was the norm. I miss that, so I put together this plan where I intend to have two funerals. The first one is obviously going to be faked because I'm not going to be dead. For the first one, I'm going to be in a rented coffin playing dead till I have the opportunity to scare the s—out of someone and then I'm going to join the wake party. I can visit with everyone just like everybody else and maybe turn it into a barbecue with beer, tater salad, Bush Beans, (or Yam beans) and whatever. Also, I'll get to see who came to my funeral and who didn't. Makes sense to me and all it will cost is the rented coffin and the food. Bring your own beer.

Could be also that if you came to the first funeral, you may be excused from the second and real one. I won't be counting heads at the second one, that's for sure. You come or don't and I aint going to know. Actually, considering heaven and all, maybe I will know. You better come again just to be safe. I intend to be in heaven, and in case you don't know, luck comes from heaven, both good luck and bad luck. I'll be keeping a list and checking it twice.

Now this is all just a tall tale and probably aint going to happen because of what happened one night at a dinner reception. My wife was visiting with a lady at the end of the table where we were sitting. I overheard them talking about funerals, so I asked what they were talking about. Seems as how my wife was telling this two-funeral story and letting her know how stupid she thought it was. Turns out this lady was a funeral director. She told my wife to bring me to her on the first funeral. She said she would cremate me so that I wouldn't be scaring anyone and would not need a second funeral. I can't tell you the name of that lady (Sarah Suret, a Voodoo woman from New Orleans, comes to mind) or the funeral home where she works, but you can bet your boobies I aint going there for the first or any of my funerals.

My advice is that you might consider being real dead before your funeral. Funerals aint funny and shouldn't be messed with. I still want to do it though. Be careful if you come to my funeral; don't get too close to the coffin, and bring beer just in case.

# Voodoo Woman

South Louisiana, Cajun country, is a different place than most people have ever experienced. It is in fact a part of the state of Louisiana and Louisiana is part of the United States, but things are different there. The land is not so much different than other parts of the world, but the people are different. Now this is not to say that there aren't other unique places in the world and different people, but this story is about very special Cajun people called voodoo women. This story is true if you want it to be. Maybe not so true if you require DNA, fingerprints, and stuff like that for proof.

Just south of New Orleans is a nest of voodoo women. Yes, a nest. It's not the only place voodoo women (or more properly voodoo priestesses) come from, but it is the source for all United States voodoo women. If you want a voodoo woman, you got to go there. Now, just to get the technical issues behind us, yes, there are voodoo men (or more properly voodoo priests)—how else you going to make new voodoo woman? The men, however, are apparently couch potatoes and no real threat to anyone. The voodoo women, by the way, come in all types. Some are scary and mean as hell and some are just fun loving and conniving menaces. These fun-loving ones will tickle a kid in kindergarten class, stick pins in a girl's butt during a serious math class, make men fart in church, and all such stuff as that. Ever have something like that happen to you that you couldn't explain? It probably was a loosey-goosey voodoo woman.

This story is about Sarah Suret, just such a voodoo woman, a conniving and fun-loving menace. Sarah was the typical young voodoo woman—slim, long black hair, black eyes, but still good looking and always smiling like she knew something about you, which she normally did. She lived by herself in a small shack out in the swamp south of New Orleans. Don't know the story on her husband, but this is typical; seems most voodoo women live by themselves. Could be like the black widow spiders; they kill and eat their mates as soon as they no longer need them. Anyway, one day when Sarah was working her spells, she got caught up in a disturbance in New Orleans and got arrested. As soon as they started checking her in with fingerprinting and such, they discovered she was a voodoo woman—you see, voodoo women don't have fingerprints. The New Orleans police called the sheriff since this was bigger than a city affair. The sheriff picked her up and put her in the county jail.

Remember Sarah was conniving, so this was not going to be a problem for her. They never did burn witches or voodoo women in Louisiana, so she had no reason to be really scared. The sheriff, however, did not share her assessment of the affair and being a mean, old SOB, he began to threaten Sarah. Of course, Sarah was kin to other voodoo women, some of which, as stated above, were scary and mean as hell. Pretty soon, the sheriff was the one that was scared and began to negotiate with Sarah.

Sarah had a very unusual request: she wanted to be the governor's wife, first lady of the state. The sheriff said heck, I can't do that and in any case the governor already has a wife. Sarah said I don't mean the current governor, I mean a future governor, and I can take care of marrying him if you will just stay out of the way. The sheriff agreed to the deal but wanted to know just why Sarah wanted to be the governor's wife. Sarah partly explained by reminding him that she was basically a good voodoo woman and she wanted to help solve a crawfish problem in the South. Of course, he had more questions, but she finally cut him off and said just hide and watch.

By and by, it finally happened. Sarah was in the state capitol as wife of the current governor. She was the state's first lady. Now the fact that she was a voodoo woman was no real secret except maybe to the governor. Governors in Louisiana are not typically smart, and remember she could do spells. Be that as it may, the Cajuns thought it was cool and loved the idea of a voodoo woman sleeping with the governor. Yankees in Louisiana (citizens living north of the current location of interstate highway I-10) didn't think much of it, but they didn't have the vote.

Now the setting for this was a long time ago, back when the interstate highway system was just getting started. Up till then, Highway 90 was not only the way across the state but it also was the defining border between Cajun country and the rest of Louisiana—not a thin line but an area of gradual conversion from one way of life to another. The highway was, however, a two-lane thin line and that was the source of the crawfish problem. You see, crawfish move about at night looking for crawfish food, whatever that is. On some warm nights, some of them would crawl long distances for this food. Some could do this and some couldn't. The difference was the weight of the crawfish. The skinny ones could crawl long distances and the fat ones couldn't. This and the two-lane Highway 90 set up a natural evolution that was going to ruin the crawfish as a food source. You see, crawfish, being very small to begin with, need to be fat to be a good meal; skinny crawfish aint worth the trouble. So now you see the problem is this: the crawfish that can make long crawls at night are the skinny ones and they are the ones that wind up crossing Highway 90. The fat ones usually never see Highway 90. Now if Highway 90 was wide enough, which it wasn't, none of the skinny crawfish could make it across before a car turned them into a greasy spot on the road. So with a wide road, if the skinny ones can't make it across the road, then they don't live to reproduce, and so they can't make any new, skinny, long-crawling, and worthless crawfish. I bet you are about to guess the answer to this problem and what Sarah did to solve the bad crawfish evolution problem.

You guessed it: she made the governor get Interstate-10 built with four lanes. Notice also (check out a map) that for her Cajun friends, she claimed a big chunk of new Cajun land from Lafayette to New Orleans. Remember where Sarah came from? And that's how Interstate-10 got across Louisiana and why south Louisiana crawfish are still fat.

Don't believe in voodoo women? Check out the Internet. You can even buy made-to-order spells. A luck spell, by the way, is going for $79.95 nowadays.

# Weather Scares

Being an outdoor person and having a wife that, early on, liked me enough to do stuff I wanted to do, we with our kids did a lot of camping. We started with a borrowed nine-by-nine tent sleeping on the ground with four babies. Being outdoors, you get to see weather up close. Up-close weather can be very scary, trust me on that. The following are stories of some of our weather scares, starting with the nine-by-nine tent.

## Garner State Park, Texas

We were camped in the park near the Frio River one night when a storm was forecasted to come through the park. The park rangers came to ask us to move into a cabin till the storm blew through. As they approached, they saw a skunk lying beside the tent basically up against where I was lying down inside. It was cold, and I guess the skunk was getting warm lying close to me. Now I know what you are thinking about a skunk willing to sleep with me. In any case, we didn't even get to the cabin before a large tree fell and blocked our path. But we went around and were saved, and the skunk actually didn't do its thing, so we got to the cabin smelling okay. Next day, the oldest boy fell into the ice-cold Frio River, making me take a very cold swim. If trouble was possible, he was willing.

## Garner State Park, Texas

Later when we owned a pop-up camper, we went back to the same park. During the night, it began to rain. I mean, it really rained. Having been drinking beer all day, I went to bed early. Sometime later in the night, my wife woke me up concerned about the rain. Still enjoying the beer, slightly drunk, I couldn't seem to take the situation serious enough for her. Finally, I asked her to look out the door and see which way the water was running. She indicated that it was running toward the river. I said okay, that's no problem. Wake me up if the river gets full and the water starts running the other way. Remember in the first story what I said about when she used to like me? Well.

## Inks Lake, Texas

This isn't really about weather but it is a camping story I want to tell. It's a very short story about what could have been a tragedy but wasn't. We were camped at the park during the summer when it was warm, so we planned to enjoy the water at a small waterfall in the park. Notice I didn't say swimming because my wife could not swim and all four of our babies were too young to know how to swim. None, however, including my wife, were afraid of the water. I never understood that about my wife, not being afraid of the water like most people that can't swim. Later, she secretly took swimming lessons and learned to swim. Back to the park story, we had never been in the water at this waterfall so we did not know about how slippery the big rock was near the bottom of the water fall, just above a big water hole. We went down to look and as soon as the first baby boy hit the slippery rock, in he went into the eight-foot-deep water hole, then another fell in. My wife was next, going after the two babies even though she couldn't swim. Before I could do anything, the other two babies slipped into the hole. My entire family was drowning. Of course I jumped in and started chunking wife and babies out of the hole, with my wife grabbing and holding on to the ones out while I got the rest. Needless to say, that was an exciting morning and a lucky day for all of us. I guess if there is lesson here it is to check out the swimming hole before letting the nonswimmers get there first, and don't let a nonswimmer near any water without a good swimmer near to help if necessary.

## Sam Rayburn Lake, Texas

We were camped in a pop-up camper during the summer. It was hot. The camper did not have air conditioning so we were late getting to bed, waiting for it to cool off enough to sleep. We were on a small strip of land that went out into the lake, and our camper was very close to the edge of the water overlooking the lake. Our boat was in the water next to our camper. Through the window, my wife saw some lightning. I remembered my dad telling me as a kid about distant lightning without sound being "heat lightning". So that's what I told my wife, not to worry, it's just heat lightning. I won't live long enough to not be reminded by my wife of that stupid statement. Later that night, the weather started getting bad, and then it got real bad. The wind started blowing so hard I thought the camper was going to blow over. We tried to get out and get into our car but couldn't because I couldn't get the door open against the strong wind. The door had a canvas cover held with Velcro straps inside to shed the rain, but it kept flying up, so I tried to hold it closed. My daughter, about a fifty-pound little girl, was helping me by holding onto the bottom of the flap. The wind would blow and pick her up off the floor so I put both of my feet against the bottom of the flap to help hold it. Later my daughter asked me how I did that with my hands pushing on the top of the door and my feet off the floor pushing on the door flap; we still today don't know how that was possible. My wife and the other kids were naturally scared; my daughter and I were too busy to be scared. Next morning when we could get out and see what the storm did, we were shocked and surprised we survived. An eight-inch-diameter tree just three feet from our camper door was gone, twisted off at about six feet above the ground. Our boat was on dry land, completely out of the water. The marina at the park was destroyed along with most of the boats that were in it. The restrooms had large trees on top of the roofs; no idea from where they came. We spent the rest of the day digging a new canal to float my boat back into the lake. I have spent the rest of my life taking flak from my wife about heat lightning. That was another outdoor near-disaster for us, but we kept on going camping.

## Ogden, Utah

This was one of our motor-home trips with another retired couple. We had been everywhere and were real experienced campers. We had stopped at a campground in Ogden, Utah, early that day and decided to eat outside on a picnic table that afternoon. The lady in the other motor home had cooked a pot of soup and was bringing it out to the table when my wife started trying to get our attention. She was looking at a tornado in a field about a quarter mile from us. The other lady grabbed the soup, put it back in her motor home, and came out telling us what we should do. She said don't get in a car and don't get in the motor home. Fine, except she didn't say where to get. We did not have a plan for a tornado, so we were practically panicked, not knowing what to do. I finally told my wife to get inside the motor home bathroom and I decided to set in the driver's seat and hold on to the steering wheel. Pretty soon, my wife came out of the bathroom. I asked her why she did that and she said she couldn't see. So you want to watch yourself die? Finally, the weather calmed and the tornado went away without anything bad happening to us. We came out of our motor home to see the other couple doing their thing. Picture this: he was sitting in his pickup truck on the passenger side with the door open, she was standing on the ground with her head in his lap. One might suppose that she was kissing his butt goodbye, I guess. Surviving this ordeal taught me a valuable lesson. You need a plan for a tornado. We had two vehicles each of which could easily outrun a tornado, and we didn't think about getting in either one and simply driving away. We have a plan now for the next one.

## Perry, Georgia

We went in our motor home to a swap meet in Perry, Georgia, in the early spring season. Not a real smart thing to do because that place is not safe in the spring of the year. First day, my wife went with me to the man-stuff swap meet. Soon, I pointed out to her how I had saved six dollars off our home price on something I had just bought. My wife being much smarter than me, said we spent over a thousand dollars on gas to get here and back so you could save six dollars? I mean, that's pretty smart thinking on her part. What could I say? That night, however, I got the chance to show my smarts. We were watching TV and a storm warning alert came on, indicating a tornado that had just killed five people was headed for our campground, and only five miles away. The campground owner came to tell us to get into the office building rather than stay in the motor home. Not me. I exercised our plan; we got the two dogs and got in our car and drove away. We stayed away out of the rain part of the storm till it was all over. When we got back everything was okay, the storm broke up before it got to the campground. Our plan worked. If you don't have a plan, you need one. Don't even think of hiding in a bathroom when you can simply drive away. Obviously, you will need to know which way to drive—probably shouldn't get in a car if you don't know which way to go.

## Hurricane Rita

Our motor home theoretically provides a perfect hurricane evacuation option. I say theoretically because as you will see in this story and the next, it can be misused and may not be so good an option as one might expect.

Rita was, early on, forecasted to come on shore about two hundred miles west of us. Ordinarily, we would evacuate to the west because the hurricanes typically move east after coming onshore, but in this case, doing so would likely put us in the path of the storm, so we went east about a hundred miles. Three hundred miles away from forecast—got to be good, right? We spent the first night in a state park, and next morning they closed the park and kicked us out. Next night we spent in the country front yard of friends, but I didn't like the open exposure so we left that spot the next morning. All the while, the storm is moving east following us. Finally, we settled down in a pocket park fifteen miles east of Woodville, Texas—lots of protection from trees and still a long way east of the storm. Along comes a young volunteer fireman trying to tell me to move because of the pine-tree danger. Being more than twice his age, I informed him that I had been dodging hurricanes longer than he had been living; we were not moving again. Now comes the hurricane, and guess what? It comes ashore practically dead south of where we are camped. No problem; by the time it gets to us, it will be about fizzled out, right?

Our camping group included my daughter and son-in-law with their pop-up camper, two grandsons, and one single son with his pickup truck which was out of gas—he gave his gas to his brother so he could leave our party. This lack of gas in one vehicle, with none available, kept us from leaving, as well as me not wanting to move again. The hurricane came to us during the night and it had not fizzled out. Everyone finally wound up in our motor home with the wind blowing and limbs falling, and it got kind of scary. Finally, everything got real quiet and the wind all but stopped. Smart me, I said, we are in the eye of Hurricane Rita; here's opportunity. We all had to pee, so the men went outside to pee in the eye of a hurricane. My advice here and now is don't try this at home. Rita did not like what we did and when the other side of the storm came, it was much worse. Limbs were falling again and then I heard a very loud noise; I knew this was not going to be good. A very large pine tree broke off about ten feet above the ground and fell onto the driver's seat of the motor home. My son-in-law was in the seat and nearly got crushed. At that time, there were seven adults and four pet dogs in the motor home, all wanting out. We did get out and into two cars and moved to the road away from the falling trees. We survived, but the motor home didn't. We were, however, able to spend the next night in the motor home with everything working, running off the generator. The motor home wasn't going anywhere though with a three-thousand-pound tree on it. Next day, all the homeless wasps and bees took up residence in the open motor home (the windshield was missing), so we had to leave.

I called the insurance agent and they said they would take care of getting the motor home out of the woods. Three times during the next week, a wrecking company guy would call me to get directions. When I asked him about the tree, he said what tree? Finally the Forest Service cut the tree off the motor home so it could be moved. They called me one morning at about 9:00 AM to tell me the tree had been removed. The same day at about 2:00 PM they called me to get permission to remove the tree—our government doing the best they can. The only thing I did smart in that whole adventure was not telling that young kid that I was a professional engineer. I'm sure, however, that his story about my smart-aleck response to his good advice is good enough without the engineer part. You know, he came back to that park after the storm to see that tree lying on top of the motor home. I bet his story about Rita is better than mine.

## Hurricane Ike

I'll make this one short, but it does have a part worth telling. Again, we wound up in a place not far enough from the ultimate hurricane path. We were in a campground in northern Houston, away from the potential high waters but not away from the high wind. We knew the owners of the park, so they told us, along with some of our kids and a few other folks that they were going to close the park but we could stay. They said if the storm got bad enough, we could go into the concrete block restrooms and be safe. The storm came at night and then the park electricity went off. No problem, we just started up the generator, and even with the TV antenna lying down, we were able to watch local TV. My wife and I discussed going to the restrooms and this is what she said: When it's your time to go, it's your time to go. If it's my time, I'd rather be in the motor home watching TV than lying on a cold restroom floor. So everybody else went to the restroom and we stayed in the motor home. It was our time to have an exciting night, and a lot of rolling and shaking going on but it wasn't our time to go. So we didn't go.

Next hurricane, we are going to evacuate to a city that doesn't have Texas as its last name.

# Work Fun

Working in an office, I think, has an unnatural effect on your mind. Maybe potentially, being descendants of monkeys, we are not supposed to be inside. In any case, most offices I have worked in have had other than normal business activities. In the office I'm about to tell about, we had about five people in the drafting room and a few bosses in private offices.

At the risk of revealing what kind of office it was, I must tell you that our drafting had to be done in ink. I mean wet ink, and without the benefit of first doing it in pencil then tracing over it. This wet ink could be a problem if you lost control of any of the ink sources. So the challenge was to see if you could make this happen to someone else without being caught and blamed for the disaster.

During our idol moments, we learned a neat trick one day that turned out to be very useful for office pranks. To make an instant firecracker, take a regular firecracker, cut the fuse off, and insert a very fine, twisted wire pair into the fuse hole. Then take the two ends of the twisted wire pair and insert them into the two contacts (plug holes) of a long electrical extension cord. Now, the twisted wire pair can be made to instantly burn by plugging the extension cord into any 120-volt electrical outlet. The instant burning of the wire acted as a very short fuse for the firecracker; thus, instant firecracker. Now with this neat office weapon, many exciting things can happen.

In case you have never seen a drafting table, it looks like this: Start with a flat-top table supported by a stack of drawers on each side, leaving an opening in the underside middle for the user's legs and stool. Then on top you have a large board that is hinged in the front where the user sits and rotates up as required by the user. Usually, the top is tilted so that the back, farthest from

## True Story, I Swear It - Maybe

the user, is about eighteen inches higher than the front, making a kind of V shape, with the small V section basically at the belly of the user. Sound interesting?

You get the picture? There is a small area near the belly of the draftsperson that cannot be seen by the draftsperson while he or she sets at the drafting table. The next ingredient in this plan is a big lunch and a quiet afternoon in the office. More often than not, this is a recipe for someone going to sleep while lying over their drafting table. Need I say more? Even a church deacon couldn't pass up this opportunity.

So some time when the potential victim was away, we would put the instant firecracker in the appropriate spot in the V section of the table and run a hidden extension cord to some remote location. The remote location was at one of our desks so that at the right time, we plugged it in and un-gently woke the poor unsuspecting soul. Obviously, as you might guess, this trick once revealed was difficult to repeat. No problem; we found other new ways to get the job done.

For example: one day, it was my job to set the trick up while everyone but me went out to lunch. I was to set the firecracker at the desk of a fellow that we had spared for some time. You see, time alone provides opportunities, and even if you know about instant firecrackers, you don't deal well with one going off inches from your belly while you are asleep.

The setup was to bring the business end of the extension cord to just behind the seat of the guy that was going to plug it in when the potential victim went to sleep. The wall outlet was just below and beside a bookcase behind the fellow that was going to plug it in. And then it happened—the potential victim came back from lunch early and caught me setting him up. No problem, just a minor change of plans. We together set up everything as planned with one major exception. Everything that could be seen looked normal. However, there were other parts of this prank that were unseen. Yes, you could see the extension cord on both ends of the plan and obviously the firecracker was disguised so as to be unseen. There was however, after we finished, another unseen firecracker; it was under some Kleenex inside the Kleenex box on top of the bookcase behind the desk of the fellow who was going to plug in the cord. The extension cord, actually another one, was connected to this firecracker rather than the one under the planned victim's desk. Sure enough, when the time came, the planned victim in this case faked going to sleep and the cord got plugged in. The fellow that did the dirty work leaned back in his chair, reached down to get the plug, and in doing so placed his face about six inches above the Kleenex box. We hadn't anticipated this and we couldn't stop it, so when he plugged in the cord, the box exploded and he was showered with shredded Kleenex. Needless to say, I nearly got my butt whipped over that, but it was funny and a classic use of the instant firecracker. I'd do it again.

Now you might wrongly think we didn't work and were being paid for just goofing off. Not so. You see, office work, for outside people, can get to be very boring. If we couldn't find some ways to break up the monotony, we couldn't get any work done. We worked and got the jobs done or we simply would have been fired.

We, however, finally got caught doing this firecracker thing and had to stop it. You would never guess how we got caught, so I'm going to tell you. Our office was a portion of a larger building that had other tenants. One tenant that shared a common wall with our drafting room was a radio broadcast station. One day, our bosses came back from lunch and told us a story about how the radio station next door, that they were listening to in the car, announced that the exploding noises, gunshots, that their audience was hearing on the radio were coming from next door where they were working on a Gunsmoke show. Oops.

Change of plan. Imagine plopping you butt up on a drafting stool that has a wood pencil in the adjustable pinhole that is supposed to have a steel pin. A sudden drop of about four inches that stops your heart and reduces your backbone length by about one-quarter inch.

In my entire working career, we (me and them other fools) got lucky and never sent anyone to an emergency room, but looking back I can see why we need emergency rooms. If you know me and are anywhere close to me, don't assume anything. If I'm still alive and well, I'm still having fun.

# X Stuff

The title here has nothing to do with this story. The X is so that this will be the last story in the alphabetical listing of the contents.

Following are a few very short stories that would not qualify as a chapter story but may be worth printing anyway.

1) A really bad dream. Can you imagine the horror of dreaming that you are falling out of an airplane for the second time? I mean, the odds of surviving that twice are, I'd say, zero. You know you are going to die, no question about it. I have had that dream.

2) One day, when I was about sixteen years old, I was working at a drive-in theater painting with green paint, dressed only in a bathing suit or shorts. Needless to say, I had green spots of paint all over me. Later in the day, I suffered what was later diagnosed as a strangulated hernia. I'll let your mama explain what that is and how painful it can be, as well as life threatening. This sent me to the hospital through the emergency room, and during the late evening I had emergency surgery. As I was being examined in the emergency room, I heard about the potential for an operation just before I passed out from pain. About three in the morning, I woke up and saw my dad at my bedside. I asked him when they were going to operate on me and he said they already did. I moved a little, the pain set in, and I knew it. Then I looked under the sheets to see myself completely naked with a very small bandage in the midst of many green paint spots. In case you don't know, emergency surgery means you don't get to clean off the green paint and you don't have pajamas to sleep in. Now back then, the assistant nurses would come to rooms with patients like me and give sponge baths and make up the bed. Sure enough, here

comes this young nurse assistant to my room. She, being very efficient and in a hurry, jerked the sheets off me to see a naked body covered with green spots. She screamed where are your cloths and what the hell is wrong with you with all those green spots? Needless to say, I was the talk of the floor for the rest of my stay.

3) Shortly after my wife and I got married, we bought a 1957 Ford V-8 with an automatic transmission. That car had a unique feature in that after automatically shifting to second gear, you could pull the gear shift handle down to low and instead of over-revving and destroying the engine, it would simple just stay in second gear till you moved the gear shift handle back up to drive. I took my wife's brother out one day to show him this neat performance trick that a 1957 Ford would do. He was just learning to drive and was occasionally driving his dad's 1955 Cadillac. I told him that the Cadillac would not do that and not to try it because it could destroy the engine or transmission. A couple of weeks later while visiting the in-laws, daddy-in-law told me his 1955 Cadillac was in the shop getting a transmission overhaul. Son-in-law was sitting on the couch about to die, knowing that I knew what had happened to the transmission. I didn't tell on him, so he lived to see another day.

4) A long time ago, before we knew benzene was a carcinogenic and that burying waste oil products would someday be a problem, work in a petrochemical plant was far different than it is today. I know this because my working career spanned that time, starting out, in the petrochemical business, as a plant operator and ending as a licensed professional engineer. I must tell you this so that you will understand that the funny story I'm about to tell is not as bad as it might sound. It happened a long time ago before everyone knew better. I worked as an operator in a small R & D pilot plant trying to develop polybutadiene, a synthetic rubber used today in automobile tires. One night, I came to work at about midnight and read the logbook orders that said to flare (burn off) the remaining liquid in the butadiene tank so it could be worked on during the next day shift. So I opened the top valve and started venting the tank. Now understand, butadiene is like the refrigerant in our air-condition systems; when you release the pressure, the stuff starts to boil and get very cold. The colder it gets, the less it boils until it just sets there like cold water and won't evaporate. That's what happened to the last gallon or so of butadiene in the bottom of the tank. I can't get the tank empty by venting. I even tried heating it with steam but it was not going to be empty by daylight. This was not going to be good for me.

To understand the end of this story, a little background information is necessary. When we started up this pilot plant, we were given some training in handling butadiene. The main concern was that under certain conditions, butadiene would chemically change to a new chemical similar to dynamite. Not theory—it really happened later in another chemical plant, blowing metal parts all over the adjacent city. So I was concerned but not really afraid. I had been working in the plant for about a year at that time; no explosions so far.

Now back to the gallon of cold boiling butadiene in the bottom of the tank. I decided to open the bottom valve and empty it into a bucket, which I did. I now have a bucket of ice-cold boiling butadiene that I surely can't get caught with when the day shift, with all the engineers, shows up. The pilot plant was located in a large open field with high clover behind the control building; it was a hot spring morning. Are you starting to guess what I did? I went behind that building and dumped that bucket, like you would a pan of wash water, into that hot clover. Remember this was before daylight and it was dark behind the building. One gallon of butadiene instantly evaporated with a very loud exploding sound. I thought I was dead. To this day, I have never been as scared as I was that morning. Unfortunately, that wasn't the end of the problem. When I came to my senses, I saw that where I had chunked the butadiene there was a large white ice patch in the clover—obvious evidence of something very wrong. I quickly got a water hose and melted the ice but, still the spot was very visible as a large patch of dead clover. I sweated out that scene for several days till the clover grew back. I did, however, follow my orders and got that tank empty for maintenance on the day shift. That's the way it was then—enough pressure to perform to cause one to break rules.

The extreme benzene exposure we endured then is another story. Thankfully, we were not lab rats or we would all be dead today from cancer caused by benzene exposure. We are smarter now, all of us, doing a lot better today and safer for it.

5) By now you have to know that what religion I have is not the norm. I do have beliefs, but mine are based on sensible, honest, and provable facts. Now I don't necessarily require scientific proof of God; instead, I recognize that God is as good an answer for our existence as any alternative science answer to date. I simply say I honestly don't know, and it doesn't make any difference because I'm going to be the best I can be in any case. I do, however, enjoy studying and debating the issue; problem is

it's hard to find anyone that is willing to honestly debate. I have read the Bible cover to cover, so I can at least talk to a preacher or priest at some minimum level of subject intelligence.

Now along came into my life an old retired Catholic priest I met through my wife's church activities. He too likes to talk and debate and is not intimidated by me. He is elderly, lives alone nearby, and needs help from time to time. I made a big mistake with him not realizing just how smart he is. We had several discussions about going to church on Sundays versus not going to church on Sundays. And I made a big point of what was really important was what you did on Mondays when the congregation wasn't looking. He agreed, and since then he makes sure I have something to do nearly every Monday. That's how I became his slave.

Thanks for buying this book and not reporting me to the sheriff or inquiring about rules for committing me to a mental facility.

Tell your stories, make someone smile, and never accept a zero day. Do something good every day.